Roger Myrick

AIDS, Communication, and Empowerment: Gay Male Identity and the Politics of Public Health Messages

*Pre-publication
REVIEWS,
COMMENTARIES,
EVALUATIONS . . .*

"**H**ow are we able to understand, analyze and ultimately resist mainstream discourse about AIDS? Anyone interested in an answer to this question cannot afford to miss Myrick's *AIDS, Communication and Empowerment*. Scholars interested in AIDS, health communication, media analysis, the rhetoric of science, and the cultural analysis of discourse will find much of interest in this well-written, theoretical analysis."

Mary Ann Fitzpatrick
*Chair, Department of Communication,
University of Wisconsin*

"**A**IDS, *Communication, and Empowerment* itself contributes to the empowerment of the critical voice in health communication scholarship. Dr. Myrick shows how symbols and meanings of/around AIDS and the gay community have become enmeshed in social power and language. Dr. Myrick's insightful cultural analyses of specific public and community health campaigns illustrates the discursive land mine that AIDS activists must maneuver. As this book shows, the way AIDS and gay people have been linguistically constructed, the historical factors that led to these constructions, the crucial need for explicit safe sex materials, and the restrictive role of government funding in conservative times all intersect to problematize AIDS information campaigns. *AIDS, Communication, and Empowerment* is a valuable book for those who wish to understand or participate in public discourse about AIDS."

Matthew P. McAllister, PhD
Assistant Professor,
Department of Communication Studies,
Virginia Polytechnic Institute
and State University

"**M**yrick's book offers an outstanding synthesis of postmodern and cultural theory applied to HIV/AIDS and then presents two compelling cases–public service prevention messages and gay community prevention efforts in Oklahoma. Scholars will find Myrick's theoretical insights useful in studying HIV/AIDS and a variety of oth-er issues that affect traditionally marginalized groups. Practitioners will find his critiques of prevention efforts useful in designing outreach efforts–and in outsmarting government constraints on prevention messages and materials. A superb and highly readable analysis of a critically important issue. I will use his theoretical foundations in my research and his analysis in my prevention work."

Nancy L. Roth, PhD
Assistant Professor,
Rutgers University

Harrington Park Press
An Imprint of The Haworth Press, Inc.

AIDS, Communication, and Empowerment

*Gay Male Identity
and the Politics
of Public Health Messages*

New, Recent, and Forthcoming Titles
of Related Interest

AIDS, Communication, and Empowerment
Gay Male Identity and the Politics of Public Health Messages

Roger Myrick

Harrington Park Press
An Imprint of The Haworth Press, Inc.
New York • London

Published by

Harrington Park Press, an imprint of The Haworth Press, Inc., 10 Alice Street, Binghamton, NY 13904-1580

Library of Congress Cataloging-in-Publication Data

Myrick, Roger
    AIDS, communication, and empowerment: gay male identity and the politics of public health messages / Roger Myrick.
        p.   cm.
    Includes bibliographical references and index.
    ISBN 1-56023-884-4 (hard: alk. paper)
    1. AIDS (Disease)–Social aspects. 2. AIDS (Disease) in mass media. 3. Gays–Identity.
    4. Health promotion. 6. Mass media in health promotion. 7. Gay men–Public opinion. I. Title.
RA644.A25M96 1996
362.1'969792–dc20   95–45914
                                                                                          CIP

For my parents and Brett, with love.

ABOUT THE AUTHOR

Roger Myrick, PhD, is Assistant Professor in the Department of Communication at Auburn University in Auburn, Alabama. He has 10 years of teaching experience in Communication, Composition, and Literature. He has published articles and presented papers on the media's portrayal of gay identity, public messages about AIDS, and media coverage of the Gulf War.

CONTENTS

Preface

This book is important to me personally because it explores a subject that both politicized me and enabled me to see the effect of public institutions on people's lives.

But more, the research I completed for this book heightened my awareness of the reality that people, often close friends and certainly myself, make up these institutions and, like it or not, participate in activities that maintain them.

This book has made me aware that one of the most dangerous culprits in the proliferation of HIV/AIDS is institutional power that exists through the process of labeling and fixing identity. This process is dangerous because it often remains invisible, and it defines who we are as individuals, groups, and cultures. While we cannot escape the process that defines who and what we are, we can strategically resist and make ironic the institutional power that drives that process.

Strategic resistance is what I have attempted in this book, and this, I think, is its strength.

I do, however, need to make two qualifications about the book's scope and focus. Most significantly, this book only focuses on one marginal group—white gay men; there is certainly good reason for this focus since they have been so hard hit by HIV/AIDS. But the people who are being increasingly victimized are members of other marginalized populations, especially African Americans and Hispanics. While the white gay response to HIV/AIDS cannot be transplanted onto other communities, I do believe that their strategies for resistance are useful for anyone whose life is being threatened by institutional processes.

It is also important that I stress that the people who are working in the HIV/AIDS industry are among the most genuine, compassionate, and dedicated people I have ever encountered. When, in the course of this book, I am critical of public health communication, it is the institutional process that bears the brunt of my criticism, not the people who are committed to enhancing people's lives through the manipulation of that process.

There are several people who provided support to me and enabled this project; I owe them a special thanks. An initial manuscript of this book served as my doctoral dissertation at the University of Oklahoma; my dissertation committee members— Drs. Lynda Lee Kaid, chair, Dan Nimmo, Gus Friedrich, Larry Wieder, and Kathleen Welch—offered valuable readings and suggestions on drafts. Dr. Betty Robbins and Nicholas Trivolidous talked with me extensively about the project and helped me develop a critical and complex perspective on the politics of communication. Dale Smithson and Dr. Larry Prater offered insight into the subject matter that sensitized me to the issues and helped me understand radical AIDS activism.

Thanks to the public health educators I interviewed for their valuable time and insight and to the editors at The Haworth Press for their encouragement and attention to detail.

Finally, my parents, Jack and Karen, have supported me in multiple ways for as long as I can remember; the completion of this project is largely due to that long-term support and love. My partner, Brett Wesner, offered multiple readings of and substantive feedback on my work. He provided me with the emotional support and the confidence to believe that what I was doing was important.

Roger Myrick

Introduction

If, as Michel Foucault argues, people are defined and constituted by what they communicate and what is communicated about them, gay identity has recently become one of the consequences of communication about AIDS. This book examines the cultural construction of gay men in light of discourse used in messages about AIDS that are often represented as educative, scientific, and informational, but that are in fact politically charged.

I first describe how national health education historically and currently stigmatizes marginal groups by associating them with images of disease and "otherness"; then I extend this research to examine how community-based education designed specifically for marginal groups often unwittingly participates in similar communicative strategies—strategies that work against the groups being addressed. Ultimately, my approach provides a critique of the politics at work in contemporary public health communication.

Aids, Communication, and Empowerment differs from traditional, quantitative communication studies. Instead, I examine the relationship between language and culture using a qualitative, cultural studies approach similar to Matthew McAllister's (1992) in "AIDS, Medicalization, and the News Media" (in T. Edgar, M.A. Fitzpatrick, and V. Freimuth, eds., *AIDS: A Communication Perspective*). There, McAllister offers a critical analysis of how communication in the form of news coverage about AIDS is made to seem scientific and thus apolitical by overemphasizing the medical elements of the story and avoiding the social implications for gays and other minorities ultimately affected. McAllister calls for communication scholars to focus more research efforts on critical studies of the political assumptions at work in AIDS messages. My work responds to this call by placing such medicalization theories in the broader context of histories of sexuality, the discursive development of contemporary gay identity, and recent public health communication.

AIDS, Communication, and Empowerment follows published research precedents set by a substantive body of scholars. My analysis is based primarily on the critical, historical analysis of discourse and sexuality offered by the French scholar Michel Foucault. I also draw on the work of:

- media and cultural critics such as Simon Watney (*Policing Desire: Pornography, AIDS and the Media*) who explore the ways homophobia fuels communication about AIDS;
- safe sex education and gay/lesbian scholars such as Cindy Patton (*Sex and Germs: The Politics of AIDS* and *Inventing AIDS*) who examine the way communication about AIDS institutionalizes marginalization of gays in the culture;
- recent and innovative work in the social science and humanities disciplines on communication by and about marginal groups, for example, R. Jeffrey Ringer (ed., *Queer Words, Queer Images: Communication and the Construction of Homosexuality*).

Ultimately, I argue that mainstream communication about AIDS and HIV relentlessly stigmatizes and further marginalizes gay identity. I further argue that even communication that originates from marginal groups often participates in linking gay identities with disease, particularly when these groups rely on funding from federal health agencies.

I conclude that governmental funding, while often necessary for the continuation of community-based health campaigns, poses obvious and direct restrictions on effective marginal education. More unexpectedly, I also find that larger cultural influences affect community-based education in insidious ways that often remain unnoticed. This significant finding allows for a radical reading of contemporary health communication that can ultimately be used to strengthen marginal voices.

To explore and argue the above, this book proceeds as follows.

Chapter 1 examines the relevant works by and about Michel Foucault, who offers an analysis of the ancient and contemporary discursive construction of sexuality and identity, and provides a theoretical foundation for understanding multiple instances of communication. Chapter 2 provides a more specific cultural context for gay identity and AIDS representations by examining recent (late nineteenth- and early twentieth- century) histories of sexuality that reveal how gay identity came to be based on issues of economics, medicine, representation, and the body. Chapter 3 focuses on more recent cultural analysts who look at AIDS as a representational disease, as well as a biological one, and provides a specific framework and context, primarily based on Foucauldian analysis, for understanding specific discourses on AIDS. This cultural analysis examines how processes of communication work to constitute, for both the queer and nonqueer, sexuality, identity, and, consequently, culture in the latter half of the twentieth century.

Chapters 4 and 5 examine specific examples of governmental discourse that work to construct cultural representations of both gays and nongays in order to show the consequence of the government's role, at both the national and state levels, in dealing with AIDS as a power issue rather than a biological one. The examples, chosen because they offer illustrative and typical indications of communication about AIDS and gays, include a national PSA campaign targeting and constituting nongay men, also known as the general public, and a statewide public health campaign targeting and constituting gay men. The former effectively silences gays, while the latter illustrates messages that speak directly to and about gays. These examples are analyzed using Foucault's approach to critical theory about communication and power.

Ultimately, I conclude that the cultural analysis of communication about AIDS and gays is useful for understanding the political consequences of public health campaigns in the 1980s and 1990s. Not only does this analysis allow for a critical reading of and resistance to stigmatizing mainstream messages designed for the general public, it also allows for a rethinking of ways marginal groups can take control of their own education on public health issues. As HIV infection and AIDS cases continue to rise dramatically among marginalized and disenfranchised groups, such analysis of health communication directed at those groups becomes crucial for survival.

Chapter 1

The Construction of the Homosexual as Subject According to Michel Foucault

Michel Foucault's critical discussion of the history of sexuality and discourse has a direct bearing and focus on the way contemporary gay identity is constructed through institutional communication, in this case communication regarding health messages about AIDS and HIV. Foucault argues that communication about sexuality that presents itself as objective, educative, and/or informational–and therefore apolitical–often constitutes discourse that presents politically charged issues as value-free truths.

Foucault argues that institutional communication creates and reinforces power relationships that define cultural identity. He develops this point by examining nineteenth-century medical discourse, which labeled nonprocreative sexuality, especially homosexuality, as deviant. Foucault's analysis offers a broad theoretical base for understanding sexuality and identity as a social construction, a move that remains crucial for understanding the politics of recent public health communication about sexuality.

FOUCAULT'S PROJECT

In order to get a clearer sense of Foucault's relevance for an analysis of AIDS messages and gay identity, the following discussion will lay out his general approaches of archaeology and genealogy as they appear in two of his central works. Fundamental to Foucault's project, and the subsequent analysis of AIDS messages, is his complex understanding of a world and culture that come to exist largely through language and power.

In *Archaeology of Knowledge* (1969/1972), Foucault establishes his understanding of the epistemology and ontology of communication by examining the relationship of language to what is taken to be knowledge and truth. By analyzing historical discourse from the time of the Enlightenment (which coincided with the rise of certain institutions, such as asylums), Foucault discerns that language enables certain power relationships and thus speaks certain institutional realities into existence. (See also Foucault, 1961, 1973, 1966/1973, 1975/1979.) In other words, it is through discourse that institutional power comes to assert itself and, thereby, to constitute its existence. This construction of "reality," the knowable, the truth, comes about through the existence of certain discursive practices, in a process through and by which subjects and objects become visible-knowable, which linguistically, through the use of lexical (metaphoric) and grammatical tropes (structural and thematic movements in language), produces possibilities for a culture. Not only does language constitute what can be known as reality for its users, but language constitutes what can be considered speaking subjects. Language for Foucault (and he draws heavily on Nietzsche's sense of language here) speaks and creates the world and its inhabitants by empowering certain people, ideas, and relationships as such. The ultimate consequence of this linguistic activity is to define, or fix, what can be taken for knowledge.

To examine the way language works, Foucault focuses the *History of Sexuality: An Introduction* (1976/1990) on an analysis of the power relationships in discursive practices that constitute sexuality and construct the self after the eighteenth century, and his analysis offers a general, theoretical, foundational context for understanding the contemporary, culturally constructed identity of gay men in the wake of the AIDS crisis. Foucault remains important here despite/because of the fact that he never wrote about AIDS, though he died of the disease in 1984.

In "The Repressive Hypothesis" (1976/1990), Foucault examines the notion that contemporaries are living in a post-Victorian, repression-free episteme, or cultural moment. His conclusion is that the proliferation of talk about sexuality in the twentieth century, exemplified later in this discussion as educative talk about AIDS, discursively works to define the self, both gay and nongay, in a position that maintains certain power relationships.

Foucault (1976/1990) begins by claiming that, with the Victorians (and this is not necessarily a starting point as much as a genealogical association), sex is transformed into discourse with the increase in the practice and manifestation of confession:

> Discourse, therefore, had to trace the meeting line of the body and the soul, following all its meanderings: beneath the surface of the sins, it would lay bare the unbroken nervure of the flesh. Under the authority of a language that had been carefully expurgated so that it was no longer directly named, sex was taken charge of, tracked down as it were, by a discourse that aimed to allow it no obscurity, no respite. (Foucault, 1976/1990, p. 20)

And the consequence?

> An imperative was established: not only will you confess to acts contravening the law, but you will seek to transform your desire, your every desire, into discourse. Insofar as possible, nothing was meant to elude this dictum, even if the words it employed had to be carefully neutralized. The Christian pastoral prescribed as a fundamental duty the task of passing everything having to do with sex through the endless mill of speech. The forbidding of certain words, the decency of expressions, all the censoring of vocabulary might well have been only secondary devices compared to

that great subjugation: ways of rendering it morally acceptable and technically useful. (Foucault, 1976/1990, p. 21)

Sexuality, and the self as constructed by sexuality, finally becomes something to be managed through discourse, and Foucault
argues that it is a proliferation of talk about sexuality, not the
repression of it, that allows for the association among control,
pleasure/sexuality, and the construction of the self. So one of
Foucault's crucial tenets is this notion that increasing institutional discourse and communication about sex in the nineteenth century allows for a situation and experience in which people become identified as a coherent, knowing self through particular
kinds of talk about sex.

According to Foucault, this has direct relevance for contemporary gay identity because, prior to the nineteenth century, same sex
desire was seen as an activity, not necessarily as something that
defined who one was. However, in the nineteenth century people
became encouraged to talk about their sexual activities as though
they revealed truths and knowledge about themselves. The person
who experiences same sex desire, or who engages in same sex
encounters, undergoes categorization, systematization by a discourse that increasingly constitutes a self as always and only homosexual: "the sodomite had been a temporary aberration; the homosexual was now a species . . . nothing that went into his total
composition was unaffected by his sexuality. It was everywhere
present in him; at the root of all his actions because it was their
insidious and indefinitely active principle; written immodestly on
his face and body because it was a secret that always gave itself
away. It was consubstantial with him, less as a habitual sin than as a
singular nature" (Foucault, 1976/1990, p. 43).

Foucault argues that the above situation is made possible and
observable because of the increasing medicalization of talk about
sexuality, a discursive situation that clearly recurs and continues in

the 1980s with associations between sexuality and disease. The medical discourse, and other kinds of discursive controls,

> function as mechanisms with a double impetus: pleasure and power. The pleasure that comes of exercising a power that questions, monitors, watches, spies, searches out, palpitates, brings to light; and on the other hand, the pleasure that kindles at having to evade this power, flee from it, fool it, or travesty it . . . these attractions, these evasions, these circular incitements have traced around bodies and sexes, not boundaries not to be crossed, but perpetual spirals of power and pleasure. (Foucault, 1976/1990, p. 45)

The construction of the homosexual in the nineteenth century then emerges not as the product of a linear power relationship between heterosexual oppressors and homosexual victims. Rather the homosexual actually enjoys the pleasure of identity through multiple experiences and moments of surveillance.

Ultimately, sexuality comes to be associated with the body and what one does with it in order to experience pleasure; as such, the body emerges as the central site for surveillance (Foucault, 1976/1990, p. 47). And the relevance here for the homosexual is that

> the implantation [or encroachment of a type of power on bodies and their pleasures] of perversions [which homosexuality is named in one way or another] is an instrument-effect: it is through the isolation, intensification, and consolidation of peripheral sexualities [including homosexuality, such as occurred in the early, and even recent, days of AIDS when it was always and only linked with gay men] that the relations of power to sex and pleasure branched out and multiplied, measured the body, and penetrated modes of conduct. (Foucault, 1976/1990, p. 48)

The homosexual, as a speaking subject, ultimately emerges as a way for power to be extended to and implanted within the body.

Contemporary sexual identity, then, can be seen as the institutional need for power to become inextricably tied up with and to the body. And in order for the body to be a part of institutional "spirals of power," and thus enjoy pleasure, it must be made visible, representable, and subject to discourse.

Thus, the homosexual voice and body, and the proliferation of medical, psychological, and familial discourse that speaks the homosexual into existence, is not about silence, but rather about endless and relentless communication and representation. Here it is important to reemphasize that Foucault's objective is to analyze a certain form of knowledge about sex in terms of power. He is not looking at the relationship of sex to power in terms of laws or prohibitions, but in terms of techniques, norms, and truth (Foucault, 1976/1990, p. 90). So it is not a question of what can/cannot be said, but which techniques of sexuality constitute power, and this is why his analysis is particularly useful for an analysis of gay men, representation, and AIDS; gay men have not simply been silenced, they have been talked to death.

In the *History of Sexuality,* Foucault charts historical changes in discourse about sexuality, ethics, and the self in order to understand the contemporary constructions of sexuality and the self that are, and have been, played out during the AIDS pandemic.

The above discussion reveals much about Foucault's main concepts. Ultimately, it is through discursive practices that subjects, objects, institutions, and knowledge come to exist; language creates what can be considered as possible. By analyzing discursive formations and linguistic practices, power relationships can be identified that are maintained through such discourse. Discursive practices have the power not only to police desire, but to constitute what that desire can be in order to maintain existing power relations.

Foucault's analysis foregrounds the cultural construction of gay identity, thus resisting and deconstructing normalizing theories of biology. This, in turn, allows for a political analysis of gay identity, or an analysis that examines the way spirals of power work to institutionally constitute what is possible, real. Furthermore, Foucault's emphasis on the body as the most recent site of the infliction/implantation of institutional power is of great importance for the following discussion. With his focus on the body, and discourse that inscribes the body, he allows for the analysis of the way language works to represent, make visible, and police gay bodies, desires, and voices. In fact, representation and visibility are two of the ways in which the culture has been able to use language to associate AIDS with gays. And given the physical ravages AIDS has wreaked on gay communities, issues of representation and the body remain inescapable. Finally and most important, Foucault's analysis of the complex ways institutional power works opens the most important space for gays. With his analysis of spirals of power that go beyond linear maneuvers, Foucault offers an explanation of identity that can be used by the marginal for their own survival. And this seems to be a strategy gays used in the 1980s to invent new possibilities for experiences and relationships that allowed them to emerge as a powerful political group in the 1990s.

NIETZSCHE AND THE ASSUMPTIONS AT WORK IN FOUCAULT'S PHILOSOPHICAL PROJECT

Foucault's most solid foundation, according to any source on the subject, is Nietzsche. Foucault is indebted to Nietzsche for both the subject of his study and the approach he used to study that subject. Mahon (1992) explains that Foucault shared Nietzsche's three main philosophical concerns: truth, power, and the subject. According to James Miller (1993), Foucault's U.S. biographer, Foucault's entire life, both personal and professional, was spent trying to fulfill his sense of a Nietzschean quest, to determine who he was and why he suffered because of who he was. And, while both Nietzsche and Foucault share what is conventionally understood as a nihilistic position with reference to "reality" and the subject, Foucault, according to Miller (1993), was completely caught up in new ways to invent the subject once the current culture was finally deconstructed, which his analysis calls for.

The notion of the opacity of language that Foucault relies on is also one that originates with Nietzsche. His understanding of language is clearly explicated by Tracy Strong (1984) in "Language and Nihilism." According to Strong, Nietzsche sees language not as the container of some hidden meaning, but as always and only constituting and maintaining the possible, the knowable. Nietzsche (1886/1981) views language (as it has developed in and constituted Western civilization) as speaking, entrapping, and creating subjects because of its figurative capabilities. Language, through the use of metaphors and other tropes, is constantly able to speak the figurative as that which is scientific. Discourse that makes use of institutional metaphors and empowers institutional subjects, and defines all in terms of institutional control, is thus able to create what seems to be a scientific and, therefore, natural/uncontestable "reality," a recurring theme in all of Foucault's work.

For Nietzsche, according to Strong (1984), language ultimately creates this uncontestable reality through the fetishization of the subject. This is accomplished through certain epistemological assumptions in which Western language participates. First, language assumes the sovereignty of the subject as an active agent that exists outside of discourse. This sovereign subject is linguistically invested with free will and the autonomous power to act on his/her best behalf, which is usually the quest for absolute knowledge/truth. Second, language, as it has developed in the West, speaks in terms of cause/effect relationships, and these relationships have been invested, culturally/linguistically, with great import: they explain, predict, and control (the traditional social scientific credo) and thus constitute "true" knowledge. As a result of these two epistemological assumptions, language remains capable of treating the subject as a natural, real entity that has control over language and its own destiny. Strong (1984) claims that Nietzsche saw language as inescapable unless people understand that they are products of and trapped by language, which seems impossible, since to speak of such entrapment would be to remain within the power and control of language (an example of Nietzschean nihilism). Nietzsche's analysis remains a striking example of the way language fetishizes the metaphoric, which becomes central to Foucault's understanding of the way power and language work to construct knowledge and identity.

Deleuze (1986/1988) claims that the real strength of Foucault is that he resists being fixed and locked into one philosophical category, such as Marxism, structuralism, or post-structuralism. Deleuze asserts that what are interesting and recurrent about Foucault are the "foldings in thought": the moments of subjectivization in Foucault in which subjectivity is simultaneously identified and deconstructed. Deleuze also responds to those critics of Foucault who claim that his analysis of power is too totalizing to offer any hope; Deleuze points out that Foucault's solution avoids humanistic liberation, but also encourages an informed opposition to the ordinary.

Foucault is a nihilist in one sense—he views the power of discourse as inescapable. But he does not stop there. He also calls for new ways to invent the self, (as Miller [1993] points out) and while he avoided saying what this might look like while he was alive, at least in academic circles, he may have discovered possibilities, according to Miller (1993), in his experiences with the eroticization of the body through sadomasochism and the new relational positions this offered.

Hunt (1992) claims that Foucault's focus on the body as the most recent site of the implantation of institutional power is his most important contribution to the study of the history of sexuality: "by focusing on bodies, Foucault offered perspectives that help disengage us from a dreary, repetitive, totalizing history of patriarchy and misogyny" (p. 82). This emphasis on the body, sexuality, and power would seem to make Foucault a logical theorist to use in order to understand contemporary messages about AIDS. However, Butler (1992) claims that Foucault's emphasis on power as productive denies death in a postmodern, technological, post-plague world, and his analysis, therefore, cannot account for AIDS. But according to Miller (1993), one of Foucault's central driving forces in his personal as well as professional life was to achieve an erotic union of life and death; to this end, he found creative pleasure in sadomasochistic experiences in San Francisco. Such an ability to create sexual experiences that resist and/or make ironic institutional life certainly seems to run counter to Butler's understanding of Foucauldian analysis as humanistically life-affirming and death-denying. Foucault's analysis of sadomasochism will be discussed in more depth later in relation to his reading of contemporary gay political movements.

To enact his focus on the body, self, power, knowledge, and discourse, and his rejection of the Enlightenment, Foucault used methodological/theoretical approaches of archaeology and genealogy, and at different times in his life and in different works these approaches received varying degrees of emphasis. Dreyfus and Rabinow (1982) offer the clearest description of these two terms:

> It is necessary, Foucault seems to be arguing, to look at the specific discursive formation, its history, and its place in the larger context of power in order to be able to evaluate its claim to describe reality. Whether we are analyzing propositions in physics or phrenology, we substitute for their apparent internal intelligibility a different intelligibility, namely their place within the discursive formation. This is the task of archaeology. But since archaeology has bracketed truth and meaning it can tell us nothing more. Archaeology is always a technique that can free us from a residual belief in our direct access to objects; in each case the "tyranny of the referent" has to be overcome. When we add genealogy, however, a third level of

intelligibility and differentiation is introduced. After archaeology does its job, the genealogist can ask about the historical and political roles that these sciences play. If it is established that a particular discursive formation has not succeeded in crossing the threshold of epistemologization, then archaeology has freed us to shift to the question of what role this pseudoscience, this doubtful science, plays in the larger context. (Dreyfus and Rabinow, 1982, p. 117)

To reduce the above, archaeology enables the analysis of how language works to constitute subjects and knowledges through discourse, and genealogy provides a historical framework for understanding how certain subjects and knowledges emerge as possibilities during certain cultural periods.

Foucault enacts this analysis on various discursive formations in Western culture: medical discourse of sanity and health, social scientific discourse of learning, legal discourse of prisons, and, ultimately, ethical discourse of sexuality. Foucault's later works emphasize the genealogical approach, or his connections between discourse and a decentered historiography, more than his earlier, more structural and archaeological approaches, which focus primarily on power relationships constituted through discursive formations.

Foucault's archaeological and genealogical focus offers a twofold advantage for the communication researcher looking at contemporary messages about AIDS and gay identity. First, his analysis of discourse and the way it works to form subjectivity and knowledge allows for the analysis of discursive practices in messages about AIDS and the consequential construction of gay identity through language. Second, his genealogical analysis of the history of sexuality provides a framework for understanding how a person historically comes to be understood in terms of sexuality and what this says about a culture's concerns and priorities.

APPLICATION OF FOUCAULT'S THEORY

The political scientist and communication scholar M.J. Shapiro offers an example of what a Foucauldian analysis would look like for the social scientist. Shapiro (1984) examines what is purported to be a descriptive statement from an FBI agent that explains certain actions that he has taken on behalf of the governmental institution. By examining the various legal/societal discourses that are juxtaposed within the statement, by analyzing certain grammatical structures that empower the speaker as a "natural speaking subject," and by pointing to metaphors that are used descriptively rather than figuratively, Shapiro offers a compelling argument for the way the agent's discourse speaks himself and his agency into indisputable being.

Schecter, in *AIDS Notebooks* (1991), offers a more exhaustive and relevant argument based on Foucault's analysis about the discursive practices at work in talk about the homosexual in the age of AIDS. Schecter enacts a loose ethnography that focuses on multiple organizations, educational approaches, and social situations that constitute gay identity in two ways: first, as a species who is nothing more than his/her sexual orientation, an alienating and modern position according to Schecter; second, as a species who is ultimately driven toward death because of his/her existential positioning as a nonprocreative sodomite, a fragmented, postmodern situation. But most interestingly, the homosexual is seen as a subject only through discourse about his/her sexuality, and with institutional, dominant discourse about AIDS, the homosexual is simultaneously denied access to this discourse and ultimately written into silence. Schecter explains:

> Before, when sex was so central to the gay experience, so much of the social discourse focused on sexual stories. Now that AIDS has made sexual adventures potentially lethal, conversation about sexual exploits tends to raise eyebrows and questions concerning the raconteur's grasp of reality or

sense of responsibility. The discourse even among gays has shifted, and what is significant about this shift is not only that AIDS has closed the horizon on the discourse about sex, but also that the discourse about sex as metaphor has receded far into the background . . . It was a fate common to the entire social movement of the sixties and seventies, where precisely that which had identified the epoch as transformative for its members, the possibility of a new social order, had withered into anything but that. A decade or so later the promise of a redefined community itself became a metaphor for that which is absent, and indeed, today society presents itself, in Hegelian terms, as absence . . . this is the context in which AIDS appears and wreaks its ravages. Where once there was a sense of community, now there is silence . . . outcasts, lepers even, which takes the peculiarly modern form of a well-nigh unbearable solitude. (Schecter, 1991, p. 25)

Schecter identifies the space for the homosexual in all of this as a dovetail between personal psychology and organized alienation, a community organized around absence (1991, p. 26).

This absence can be seen in the predicament in which gays find themselves. According to Schecter, the culture encourages gays to talk about their sexuality and ways of managing AIDS; but their talk, their discourse, must be emptied of sexuality, given the cultural link between gay sex and death, and incorporated into medical discourse that promotes management of the self as pleasurable. Of course, when the homosexual must speak him or herself with discursive practices that work to marginalize and identify the homosexual as a "species," the homosexual becomes fixed into a position that identifies him/her as other; at the same time the culture denies the homosexual the space to unite sexual orientation with sexual acts, which is what defines the homosexual as "difference" initially; without the ability to speak of sexuality, the homosexual is at once other, but denied the status, the voice of other (Schecter, 1991, p. 63).

As a consequence of this paradoxical positioning, Schecter claims that homosexuals, and not just those with HIV or AIDS, have stopped talking and begun waiting. He tells a story of a man who goes to a gay bar where he is engaged by another man who wants to go home with him. The first man, the one being propositioned, wonders "about the fantasy if AIDS were not there to disrupt it" (Schecter, 1991, p. 118). The first man finally goes home alone because he decides there will be little to say after the proposed lovemaking, and "one makes love in order to speak" (Schecter, 1991, p. 118). So "he waits, does not talk" (Schecter, 1991, p. 118). Foucault might respond to Schecter by reminding him that even such absence is part of the discourse that surrounds and constitutes the presence of the disease and the gay subject.

CONCLUSION

Foucault's reading of the cultural and discursive construction of identity, sexuality, and the body in relation to spirals of institutional power makes his analysis of the contemporary construction of homosexuality imperative for a discussion of cultural communication about AIDS. In fact, recent cultural theorists looking at contemporary and historical histories of sexuality and the construction of the homosexual within those histories remain heavily reliant on Foucault for their analysis. In the following chapters, the reader will get a sense of how Foucault's analysis of identity and sexuality played out before and after his death, and a sense of the importance of his analysis for the understanding of gay voices at work in discourse about AIDS.

Chapter 2

Recent Histories of Sexuality and Their Relevance for Gay Identity

Foucault's *History of Sexuality* stops short of making explicit associations with sexual politics occurring after Freud; it also fails explicitly to consider gay and lesbian politics of recent times, a logical extension of his critical history of sexuality and a crucial factor in understanding current communication about AIDS and HIV. In this chapter I extend Foucault's analysis to understand the development of the modern-day gay and lesbian liberation movement, which provides a context for the complexity of public health messages about AIDS.

What remains particularly interesting about this history of sexual politics is that it illustrates a phenomenon Foucault called "reverse discourse," or a move in which a group that has been culturally positioned as "other"–a position that obviously limits the group's power–reverses the cultural meaning of such communication and uses it as an organizing principle of positive identity and empowerment.

The ultimate thesis of this chapter argues that the power of the contemporary gay and lesbian civil rights movement and its politics of difference lies in its ability to communicate about and represent the body, desire, and sexuality as diverse through a critique of institutional power. Such communicative power is largely responsible for educational messages that have enabled this marginal community's survival.

This chapter will begin with a focus on recent discourse theories on the history of sexuality, with a foundation in Foucauldian analysis; these theories provide a historical context and point of reference for the development and progression of what has been called the gay liberation movement in the United States during the twentieth century. Ultimately this chapter will offer the reader a contemporary cultural framework that s/he can use to make sense of the consequences of certain kinds of communication about gays and AIDS that will be explored in later chapters.

HISTORY OF SEXUALITY: LATE NINETEENTH AND EARLY TWENTIETH CENTURIES

One of Foucault's primary contributions to recent histories of sexuality has been his focus on the ability of discourse to produce pleasure and desire. Taking this as his lead, Halperin (1989/1993) provides a framework for recent cultural theories on sexuality and the formation of sexual identity. He claims that a conceptually coherent examination of sexuality would "de-center sexuality [as a fixed and given entity] from the focus of the cultural interpretation of sexual experience" (p. 424) and instead look at "the production of desire" (p. 425):

> To the extent, in fact, that histories of "sexuality" succeed in concerning themselves with sexuality, to just that extent are they doomed to fail as histories (Foucault himself taught us that much), unless they also include as an essential part of their proper enterprise the task of demonstrating the historicity, conditions of emergence, modes of construction, and ideological contingencies of the very categories of analysis that undergird their own practice. Instead of concentrating our attention specifically on the history of sexuality, then, we need to define and refine a new, and radical, historical sociology of psychology, an intellectual discipline de-

signed to analyze the cultural poetics of desire, by which I mean the processes whereby sexual desires are constructed, mass-produced and distributed among the various members of human living-groups. (Halperin, 1989/1993, p. 426)

Important here is Halperin's call for an analysis of the history of sexuality that does not take sexuality and subsequent sexual identity as a given, as a starting point, but rather as a consequence of the social and cultural construction of desire, and this is a view that is only possible in a post-Foucauldian world. This cultural constructivist approach, one taken by the historians discussed below, is crucial for an examination of gay identity in the late twentieth century because it provides a context for the representational influence of AIDS and HIV educational messages on understandings of a gay self; furthermore, this approach allows for the politicization and, ultimately, the deconstruction of dominant culture's use and construction of sexuality as identity to maintain a discursive system of surveillance and discipline.

D'Emilio and Freedman (1988) offer a look at the early history of the social construction of sexuality in America beginning with the seventeenth century; their analysis provides a historical, mainly economic perspective on how sexuality came to be and how it eventually came to define American citizens. They also offer a foundation for the formation of various discourses that become influential in the twentieth century.

According to the authors, during the colonial years, legitimized sex, not sexuality, was related to family and procreation for religious as well as economic reasons. By the end of the eighteenth century, sex was beginning to move away from the family and into the world of commerce. One consequence of this was a greater emphasis on the individual, in terms of pleasure and desire, and less on the family; in addition, sex was becoming separated from reproduction.

Consequently, the eighteenth century marked a pivotal point in the possibility for same sex love (D'Emilio and Freedman, 1988). During the colonial period, people were not existentially identified as homosexual or heterosexual, but rather as participating in acts that were either procreative or nonprocreative. However, in the nineteenth century, sexuality came into existence as a subject of discourse, homosexuality and heterosexuality were named by medical professionals, and people's identities came to be constructed on that basis. The movement away from the family and reproduction that took shape in the eighteenth century paved the way for the use of sexuality as essentially definitional for identity.

D'Emilio and Freedman (1988) claim that in the nineteenth century the changes that began in the eighteenth century coalesced as sex became more commercial and less familial, reproductive, and heterosexual, and as the opportunity for same sex love grew. In response to these cultural changes, the second half of the nineteenth century experienced a surge in public discussions of sex and sexuality in the form of anti-vice, moral, and public health/medical campaigns. The former, as the authors discuss it, offers some interesting parallels to the state's "policing of desire" seen in the 1980s, which will be discussed later:

> Two underlying themes characterized the anti-vice efforts [of the late nineteenth century] to use the state to regulate sexual expression. First, sexuality had to be restored to the private sphere; therefore any public expression of sexuality was considered, by definition, obscene. Second, lust was in itself dangerous; therefore Comstock [an anti-vice crusader of the period and namesake of the Comstock anti-obscenity laws, which are similar to the 1988 Helms' Amendment] and his allies attacked not only sexual literature sold for profit but also any dissenting medical or philosophical opinion that supported the belief that sexuality had other than reproductive purposes. (D'Emilio and Freedman, 1988, p. 160)

Not only did these anti-vice campaigners rail against prostitutes and homosexuals, they also went after women who were seeking rights outside of the familial scene. As early as the nineteenth century, then, discourse that sought to naturalize reproductive sex was proliferating in what was identified as the public realm, and one way that this was accomplished was through attempts to legislate a highly conservative sense of morality.

In addition, medical discourse was also working to reconstruct sex under the rubric of the family, by the identification and naming of perversions and perverts: "the medical labeling of same-sex intimacy as perverse conflated an entire range of relationships and stigmatized all of them as a single, sexually deviant personal identity" (D'Emilio and Freedman, 1988, p. 13). D'Emilio and Freedman claim that this move from religious to legal and medical restrictions singularly marked this century. Medical discourse engaged in surveillance of morality through public health campaigns against cholera, sex education, and the development of germ theory. In each case, doctors attempted to keep sex tied to marriage through conflation/creation of homosexuality and disease.

Key players in the proliferation of medical discourse on sexuality in the second half of the nineteenth century were the sexologists–Havelock Ellis, Krafft-Ebing, and Magnus Hirschfeld; later Kinsey and Masters and Johnson–whose conversations helped to make desire and sexuality scientific. These sexologists sought to categorize and scientize sexual behavior into binary oppositions–such as homosexual/heterosexual, abnormal/normal–in order to identify what was deviant (Niekerk and van der Meer, 1989) and, Foucault argues, to ensure surveillance of all. Thus categories of deviance were established, photographs were taken, and deviant sex and those who participated in those acts–usually nonprocreative, anal ones–became subjects to be cured or permanently hospitalized by the medical communities.

Weeks (1985) argues that what is interesting to note about the sexologists is not just that their diagnoses and binaries privileged heterosexuality and procreation; rather what is most compelling is the sexologists' compulsion for normalcy in setting up fixed categories and relationships for/among sex, gender, sexuality, identity, and the social world, and establishing these categories and relationships as truth/common sense. In the sexologists'obsession for normalcy, homosexuality became the main construction and example of the abnormal in the nineteenth century. This link between sex and truth is also central to Foucault's argument in the first volume of *History of Sexuality.*

According to Weeks, the explanatory power of the categories and relationships was what engendered sexology as a discipline and sexologists as scientists: "sexology filled a conceptual space that made it indispensable. Sexologists were not sure what sex was; but they knew that behind it lay a sexual force which explained the nature of the individual subject and his or her object choice and sexual practices" (Weeks, 1985, p. 91). Weeks (1985), following Foucault's lead, describes this as the scientification of sexuality. Not only was the study of sex capable of illuminating social relationships, sexology claimed to reveal truth about subjectivity. Thus the nineteenth- and twentieth- century sexologists provided a scientific amalgam of sex, identity, and truth.

While this medico-scientific discourse of the sexologists constructed and positioned same sex desire as deviant, paradoxically, it also contributed to the coalescing of power based on that desire. Weeks (1985) explains that certain sexologists, especially Hirschfeld, were interested in looking at and constructing alternative sexualities through an amoral perspective, in order to give voice and a certain credence to nonprocreative desire; and, in fact, the early work of the sexologists, in creating the homosexual as a speaking subject, albeit a deviant one, provided the basis for the formation of communities of people who shared that sexual identity. Weeks (1985) explains that because the categories the sexologists

used were often ambiguous and contradictory, they were also ultimately used by the disempowered against scientific communities.
Weeks (1985) points out that sexologists did not simply create
categories that then created identity; often people rejected the categories assigned to them, thus using the categories to gain new
freedoms, a move Foucault defines as "reverse discourse" (this
term will be discussed more later).

The early part of the twentieth century witnessed the emergence
of new participants in the cultural conversation about sexuality; this
contribution came from the government in the form of legislative
and political discourse that was heavily influenced by the Progressive political movement. D'Emilio and Freedman (1988) describe
one of the Progressives' first national campaigns, which dealt with
venereal disease; the authors' description sounds much like a description of the public health response in the 1980s to AIDS and
HIV: "they [the American Social Hygiene Association] advocated,
nation-wide, not merely education against venereal disease, but also
state-mandated blood testing before marriage, required reporting of
cases of infection, and a comprehensive program of sexual education that would enlist families, churches, civic institutions, and,
especially, the public schools in an effort to fashion a truly hygienic
code of sexual life" (D'Emilio and Freedman, 1988, p. 205).
According to D'Emilio and Freedman the theme of the educational
efforts was that sex should occur only within marriage, and the
culprit that caused venereal disease was male desire, more than
prostitution and homosexuality. In the 1980s, the theme of mainstream AIDS educational efforts is that only heterosexuals should
engage in sex, and the culprit emerges explicitly as homosexuality.
In both cases, people are encouraged through institutions to manage
themselves in the name of acting as educated, responsible, coherent
selves.

D'Emilio and Freedman (1988) cite the early twentieth century as the time when sexologists and Freud were also encouraging
people to talk more about sex and desire, and sexuality came to

be discussed as an integral part of identity, one's "true nature." More and more people were encouraged to view desire as intimately bound up with self-expression. While the nineteenth century constructed and talked about desire on the basis of moral (and, in the later part of the century, medical) self-control and management, the twentieth century talked about desire in terms of personal gratification based on biological, thus still medical, needs. In this atmosphere, homosexuality and its status as an identity began to be discussable in more open, though no less dangerous, terms.

While medical discourse of the sexologists and Freud helped re-present same sex desire as homosexuality, defined the homosexual by positioning him or her as aberrant, and constructed means of surveillance to monitor gays, as stated earlier, it also provided the means for gays and lesbians to gain access to communities and identities that they had been denied access to before; and, in fact, in the early part of the twentieth century, gay and lesbian communities, neighborhoods, and networks in large cities begin to proliferate. This sets the stage for contemporary identity politics and gay liberation movements. Equally as important as medical discourse is the government's increasingly influential role in the cultural discourse on sexuality and gay identity, a role that becomes more complex, pervasive, and dangerous for gays with the health crisis of the 1980s.

EARLY RUMBLINGS OF GAY AND LESBIAN POLITICAL MOVEMENTS–1950 TO 1969

The 1950s mark a watershed in the construction of gay desire and the erotic as gay and lesbian communities flourished during this postwar period (D'Emilio and Freedman, 1988). Men and women, for the first time for many, found themselves in large metropolitan cities, thrived in same sex worlds, and were unwilling to return to isolated areas where community based on gay desire was unspeakable. Beyond this geographic movement, which resulted in community-building, several other forces were at work that formed fragments of this early reconstruction of gay desire.

For the economic and political analysis of D'Emilio and Freedman (1988), 1920-1960 marks the rise and fall of liberalism, which was often based on discursive contradictions: "on the one hand, the discourse on sexuality expanded enormously, blurring the distinction between private and public that characterized middle class life in the previous century . . . on the other hand even as the erotic seemed to permeate American life, white middle class Americans struggled to maintain sexual boundaries . . . homosexuality remained beyond the pale" (p. 277, also see D'Emilio, 1993). For example, during the 1940s and 1950s, advertising, the Kinsey report on sexuality, and Supreme Court rulings on obscenity appeared liberal; furthermore, there was a concurrent Catholic-led purity movement that failed to take hold as Comstock's morality movement had in the nineteenth century because it lacked a strong connection with mainstream America (D'Emilio and Freedman, 1988).

However, one area in which controls were greatly increased was that of gays and lesbians. While the end of World War II brought a significant influx of gays and lesbians together in large urban areas in which they ultimately formed communities, the 1950s, with McCarthyism, were also a time of governmental crackdown on gays. This opened the door for local harassment that lasted well into the 1960s.

Rubin (1984/1993) understands the 1950s social control as similar to Comstock's 1880 moral crusade against certain sex acts and sexualities, as they were being defined by the medical community. Focusing on the nineteenth century, Rubin identifies prostitution and masturbation as central culprits of the period's sexual panic; interestingly, the focus is still on acts, rather than on sexualities. During the 1950s, however, "major shifts in the organization of sexuality took place. Instead of focusing on prostitution or masturbation, the anxieties of the 1950s condensed most specifically around the image of the 'homosexual menace' and the dubious specter of the 'sex offender'" (Rubin, 1984/1993, p. 5). Crusades against gays and "sex offenders" were carried out through federal, state, and local law enforcement agencies and through the medical profession, which used the government's link between the homosexual and the "sex offender" to increase "police powers over homosexuals and other sexual 'deviants'" (Rubin, 1984/1993, p. 5).

Rubin (1984/1993) identifies at least two general themes that emerge during cultural periods of sexual panic: sex negativity, or negative attitudes toward sex in general, and sexual stratification, or a hierarchical placement of different sexualities and sex acts associated with those sexualities. Marital, procreative, heterosexual sex, of course, remains at the top of the hierarchy.

The maneuvers used to enact surveillance of gays and lesbians were also accomplished through associations between homosexuality and communism. Weeks (1985) explains that during times of national peace, cultural forces turn victimizing discourse inward, at some defined internal rather than external enemy.

For example, Edelman (1993) shows how 1950s representational strategies constructed the homosexual as criminal: he explores Cold War discourse on male homosexuality by looking at representations of a 1964 sex scandal in which President Johnson's chief special assistant was arrested for disorderly conduct in a public restroom, and representations of homosexuals and their "lifestyle" that appeared at the time in popular press publications such as *Newsweek* and *Life*. Edelman understands the contemporary political and stratified nature of sexuality, which Rubin also discusses, as indicative of male anxiety about penetration and the body, which was culturally linked, in the context of 1964, to postwar U.S. fear of invasion by communists. To unpack this claim, Edelman (1993) analyzes 1950s media representations, both visual and print, of homosexual males and their communities, and through these representations identifies the move to make gays visible, easy to identify, and thus subject to surveillance. Moreover, these representations, as do 1980s representations, posited the homosexual as outwardly effeminate and thus identifiably different from heterosexual males. What is important in terms of power, though, was the focus on the body as the visible indicator, the point of difference, for "the heterosexual himself wants to believe that the gay man is, in fact, like a woman to the extent that his difference can somehow be discerned through or inscribed upon his body, thereby making him subject to discrimination in more ways than one" (Edelman, 1993, p. 559). But it was also the body, and the phallic sameness of that body for heterosexual and homosexual men, that caused profound existential, sexual anxiety for heterosexual men of the 1950s, and certainly the same argument can be made for more recent periods.

Edelman (1993) places this anxiety linguistically in the public men's restroom: "I want to suggest that the men's room, whose very signifier in this fable enshrines the phallus as the token not only of difference, but of difference as determinate, difference as knowable, is the site of a particular heterosexual anxiety about the inscriptions of homosexual desire and about the possibility of knowing or recognizing whatever would constitute the 'homosexual difference'" (p. 562). In the public restroom, Edelman argues, the cause of such anxiety about the body and the fixity of identity rested, not with the phallus, but with the private stalls in which men experienced the loss of sphincteral control. This loss left the heterosexual open for possible penetration, feminization, and ultimately the fragmentation of a fixed heterosexual identity through the creation of an "internal space of difference" (Edelman, 1993, p. 563), thus the anxiety. Edelman (1993) finally reconnects this personal, subjective fear with national concerns and fears of invasion by communists during the 1950s. Similar to that of Rubin (1984/1993), Edelman's effort results in an understanding of desire as a political construct–in Edelman's case, of postwar politics. But what is particularly exciting about Edelman's analysis is the linguistic link that he makes between representation and identity, a link that becomes crucially important when thinking about the 1980s, representations of AIDS, and the construction of male identity. According to Edelman (1993), marginal identity and the politics that construct it were/are grounded in cultural and psychological anxiety about the status of the phallus. More simply, cultural stigmatization of the homosexual was/is grounded in a fear of difference, particularly internal difference, and the resulting attempts to maintain a position of coherence by positing an external other.

Also important to the 1950s was the formation of professional and social organizations devoted to gay and lesbian orientations. As discussed earlier, after the war, gay communities began to spring up in large urban coastal areas as gays returned from the war and sought refuge among people with similar orientations. The first two homosexual organizations that formed were a lesbian group, the Daughters of Bilitis, and a gay group, the Mattachine Society, both West Coast based groups initially (Marcus, 1992). Marcus (1992) identifies an interesting shift in the Mattachine Society that can be seen as reflective of later shifts and points of emphasis in gay politics. The early version of Mattachine, begun in 1951, was started and run by Harry Hay and a group of communists who were intent on keeping the organization closed and secret in order to maintain protection for its members. However, in 1953, Hal Call wrested the organization from its original founders in order to separate Mattachine from its communist origins, thus guarding against McCarthyism, and to make Mattachine more democratic and open (Marcus, 1992). This move toward openness is a cornerstone for politics in the post-Stonewall era as being "out" becomes the ultimate and essential political statement for gays and lesbians.

Speaking of Mattachine and early gay identity politics, Weeks (1985) says this is the first time homosexuals identified themselves as a fixed group, a minority with rights. So identity as gay became an important political statement. The Mattachine saw gays as having things in common with other minorities, and this commonality was heavily stressed in the postwar years.

In sum, the 1950s gay and lesbian political movements were organized around several concerns: the liberal politics of the postwar years combined with the cultural explosion of morality in response to sexual liberation; the nation's response to peace and its fears of diversity and internal difference; economic and geographic changes that decentered the heterosexual family; the linguistic representations of the homosexual as difference, as criminal, as foreigner; and the formation of collective organizations that embody the coalescence of power.

Central to all of the above is what Weeks (1985) sees as the core of the gay and lesbian civil rights movements of the 1950s and 1960s: prior to the Stonewall riots of 1969, gay and lesbian rights movements were struggling with the questions of identity, formation of communities, and issues of representation. And these struggles simultaneously deconstructed the heterosexual family and reconstituted possibilities for new identities based on alternative sexual relationships.

STONEWALL, DISCO, AND GAY LIBERATION– 1969 TO 1980

The gay liberation movement underwent a shift in the late 1960s and began to question homosexuality as fixed, and activists started to focus on gayness as a subversive political strategy and civil right (Weeks, 1985, p. 198). Activists claimed that it was important to look at gays and lesbians as a minority, but that could not be the last word because it relied on the assumption of a preponderance and domination of heterosexuals.

Many, including Weeks, cite the 1969 Stonewall riots as the beginning of the modern-day gay liberation movement. This uprising began at the Stonewall Inn in New York City, where New York City police often conducted raids to round up and incarcerate homosexuals. During such a raid, one night in 1969, a group of female impersonators picked up bricks and stones and fought back, and the next day posters supporting the activists' efforts appeared around the city (Marcus, 1992). Weeks (1985) claims that this is one of the historical events that began to organize gay activism around the term "political."

In the late 1960s, gays and feminists were reacting against the liberal sexuality movement of the decade, one that provided sexual freedom primarily for white straight men, and the result was a reconstitution and politicization of desire for these marginalized groups: "both movements analyzed the erotic as a vehicle for domination which, in complex ways, kept certain social groups in a subordinate place in society. No longer a natural 'instinct' or 'drive,' sexuality emerged more clearly than ever as an issue of power and politics" (D'Emilio and Freedman, 1988, p. 308). Thus, in the later part of the decade, feminist and gay/lesbian organizations began to form that sought radical liberation from and voice in the midst of, heterosexual male discourse of liberalism. Two consequences of this were that the sexual became overtly political and nineteenth-century distinctions of public and private seemed to collapse.

One manifestation of this radical liberation for gays and lesbians, particularly interesting for identity politics, is the act of "coming out," or publicly asserting one's sexual orientation. D'Emilio and Freedman (1988) explain, that "coming out . . . came to represent not simply a single act, but the adoption of an identity in which the erotic played a central role. Sexuality became emblematic of the person, not as an imposed medical label connoting deviance, but as a form of self-affirmation . . . sex served to define a mode of being, both public and private, that encompassed a wide range of activities and relationships" (p. 303). Thus gay liberation after Stonewall took the construction of desire based on nineteenth-century medical definitions of homo- and heterosexual, which originally worked to control non-marital and procreative sex, and reconstructed a positive, liberationist identity based on same sex desire, a move Foucault calls reverse discourse.

Much of gay liberation in the 1970s centered around a celebration and liberation of gay sexuality, sexuality that had been constructed to be kept secret–though not silent, and under surveillance. Foucault (Gallagher and Wilson, 1984) claims that one example of the 1970s transference of the sexual into the social was the emergence of public gay bars, which before had been private. These bars constituted several facets of gay experiences: social/interpersonal, political, sexual, existential, and spiritual. In short, the bars were sites of multiple forms of interaction; gay people did in gay bars what they could not always safely do, though straight people could, outside of these bars: they became embodied selves.

One of the most visceral discourses that often constituted and permeated these bars, and gay public selves, was disco music. Hughes (1993) offers a useful, relevant, and quite Foucauldian reading of disco music as it pertains to gay experiences of identity and relationships during the 1970s:

> Disco has the power to recreate the self because the beat embodies desire. Crucial to this power is the physical sensation of the disco bass line–it is said that one "feels" the throbbing beat inside one's body, rather than merely hearing it. The oft-heard exhortations to "get out on the floor" and "get down" suggest that the power of the beat to make us dance is commensurate with the power of desire to lead us into sexual acts, even those considered forbidden, unnatural, unnameable. Desire, according to this analogy, is more

than a physical sensation or a psychological drive; it is an external force that can penetrate and establish control over any number of individuals, drawing them into a community of submission. Thus "love" is described hyperbolically as enslavement, insanity, or addiction, as disease or as police, as anything that rivals the despotism of the beat itself . . . when we allow the beat to become part of us we disturb the very foundations of conventional constructions of masculine selfhood; to allow oneself to be penetrated and controlled by music, by desire, or by another person is to relinquish the traditional conditions of full humanity and citizenship, and to embrace instead the traditional role of slave. (Hughes, 1993, p. 10)

Although Foucault never discusses the subject of disco, the above description of it as an experience of communication and identity certainly illustrates his notions of gay experience as capable of creating new understandings and relationships that constitute identity. And, for Foucault, these new relationships are spoken and represented by the gay playing-out of identity through shifting roles of submission and domination. These shifts constitute a new identity based on diversity and a throwing off/rethinking of a fixed, post-Enlightenment, monosexed self. (Foucault's analysis of contemporary gay politics and identity will be discussed in more detail in the next section.)

Weeks (1985) sees the ultimate strength of the political organization of the modern gay liberation movement that took hold during the 1970s, and continues to exist, as this questioning of the fixity of human sexuality: "by its existence the new gay consciousness challenges the oppressive representation of homosexuality and underlies the possibilities for all kinds of different ways of living sexuality. This is the challenge posed by the modern gay identity. It subverts the absolutism of the sexual tradition" (p. 201). Of course, the seeming contradiction remains: gay liberation claims that sexuality is not fixed, but, because it is an identity-based movement, gay liberation relies on a certain degree of fixedness for its very existence. Weeks (1985) accounts for this contradiction as follows: given the repressive culture, "the adoption of a gay or lesbian identity inevitably constitutes a political choice . . . they are self-creation, but they are creation . . . not freely chosen but laid out by history. . . . identity is about a way of being in the world–the making of sensibilities" (pp. 209-10). Weeks' description provides a useful, concrete explanation of the complexity of contemporary gay identity and politics and its basis in power relations: both are liberatory in a sense because they allow for the celebration of diversity, which is crucial to this movement; however, both depend upon a position of resistance to dominant discourse for their existence as coherent. On one level, what contemporary gay identity and politics represent culturally is the playing-out of spirals of power that, according to Foucault, constitute what can be taken for identity, knowledge, and truth. But the ways that gays and lesbians position themselves in relation to institutional power also creates a situation in which that power is made ironic.

FOUCAULT ON CONTEMPORARY GAY POLITICS

Regarding contemporary gay politics and Foucault, several interviews conducted with the scholar in the later years of his life deal explicitly with the deconstructive nature of such movements. Dollimore (1986) explicates Foucault's understanding in the first volume of the *History of Sexuality* of the shift in the construction of identity from nineteenth-century repression to late twentieth-century liberation for gays:

> Extrapolated, the model which emerges here is one in which the marginal and the deviant are indirectly creations, effects, of the dominant. For the radical humanist such a view

seems (understandably) to rob the marginal of its own dis-
tinctive nature, the source of its potential independence, that
authenticity which seems the precondition of it possessing
any subversive power at all, of its own. But perhaps resistance comes from elsewhere, in part from the inevitable
incompleteness and surplus of control itself. So, in the case
of homosexuality what Foucault calls a reverse discourse
develops: homosexuality begins to speak on its own behalf,
to forge its own identity and culture, often in the self-same
categories by which it has been produced and marginalized,
and eventually challenges the very power structure responsible for its 'creation.' (Dollimore, 1986, p. 180)

Contemporary gay identities and liberation movements based
on this reverse discourse and sexual diversity politically become
what Escoffier (1985), again citing Foucault, calls not a politics
of singular identity, but rather a politics of difference:

In gay politics not only has the affirmation of shared experience resulted in the consolidation of homosexual different-
ness, but in the lesbian and gay-male communities' drive
for affirmation differences have emerged among the members of both communities that cannot be eradicated. Political action eventually provokes internal conflict or splits
political movements along the most significant social fault
lines of a historical period—such as class, religion, race, or
generation. But not even an individual's identity is ever
completely harmonious or unified with itself. This is the
transgressive experience through which we discover the
limits of our membership, our real heterogeneity. Thus the
politics of identity must also be a politics of difference. The
politics of identity is a totalizing drive that attempts to uni-
versalize its norms and conduct; the politics of difference
affirms limited, partial being. (Escoffier, 1985, p. 149)

Gay identity becomes coherent then through its celebration of diversity. This later becomes a problem because, while gay communities easily celebrate diverse sexualities among white males, other kinds of diversities within gay communities are often silenced and further marginalized.

In the interviews discussed below, Foucault explains explicitly what he saw as the contribution gay politics could and did make to his critique and understanding of the history of sexuality. First, it is important to reemphasize that Foucault understands contemporary homosexual identity in terms of the word "gay," and all that the use of that word as opposed to the use of "homosexual" implies. As Dollimore (1986) points out above, the contemporary gay movement is the consequence of communities of people devoted to and stigmatized by same sex desires participating in reverse discourse in which the stigmatizing discourse is used as a positive source of identity and community. Foucault (Barbedette, 1983), claims that this reverse discourse, and its embodiment in the term "gay," also works to deconstruct the culture's binary opposition of homo- and heterosexuality:

> That's [contemporary use of the word "gay"] because by getting away from the categorization "homosexuality-heterosexuality," I think that gays have taken an important, interesting first step; they define their problems differently by trying to create a culture that makes sense only in relation to a sexual experience and a type of relation which is their own. By taking the pleasure of sexual relations away from the area of sexual norms and its categories and in so doing making the pleasure the crystallizing point of a new culture—I think that's an interesting approach. (Barbedette, 1983, p. 39)

In fact, what Foucault (Gallagher and Wilson, 1984) believes distinguishes the gay movement is its construction of a new relational culture that creates alternative possibilities for experience that resist, though never fully escape, institutional power. Foucault, in discussing the issue of sexual liberation and gay consciousness, claims that there is no such thing as a fixed gay identity that one discovers, but only the process of becoming gay: "we don't have to discover that we are homosexuals . . . rather, we have to create a gay life. To become" (Gallagher and Wilson, 1984, p. 27). Part of this becoming is "the creation of new possibilities of pleasure" (Gallagher and Wilson, 1984, p. 27), the construction of new sexualities and desires based on relationships with others that institutions do not currently sanction. Foucault sees this as the radical possibility of the contemporary gay movement: it creates spaces for new ways of being in the world.

As Dollimore (1986) says above, this ultimately sets the stage for Foucault's notion of the politics of difference. Given the relational, rather than fixed, experience of being gay, a space is opened for new relationships that people can have with themselves (Cohen, 1988), and the Enlightenment's notion of a fixed and unchanging identity is deconstructed. Foucault explains: "the relationships we have to have with ourselves are not ones of identity, rather they must be relationships of differentiation, of creation, of innovation. To be the same is really boring. We must not exclude identity if people find their pleasure through this identity, but we must not think of this identity as an ethical, universal rule" (Gallagher and Wilson, 1984, p. 28). Much of this new relationship with the self that gay politics offers lies in the use of the body for multiple pleasures.

To illustrate his notion of these new relationships gays offer among the self, others, and the body, and the creation of new pleasures and desires, Foucault (Gallagher and Wilson, 1984) turns to sadomasochism (S/M), a favorite penchant of his. S/M, as well as other gay sexual experiences that resist or problematize institutional norms, decenters the ethical emphasis institutional power and discourse place on sexual pleasure attached to genitalia, and instead treats the entire body, and its relationship to an other–either master or slave–as a source of pleasure. According to Foucault,

> it's [the recent "proliferation of male homosexual practices"] of the real creation of new possibilities of pleasure, which people had no idea about previously. The idea that S/M is related to a deep violence, that S/M practice is a way of liberating this violence, this aggression, is stupid. We know very well what all those people are doing is not aggressive; they are inventing new possibilities of pleasure with strange parts of their body–through the eroticization of the body. I think it's a kind of creation, a creative enterprise, which has as one of its main features what I call the desexualization of pleasure. The idea that bodily pleasure should always come from sexual pleasure, and the idea that sexual pleasure is the root of all our possible pleasure–I think that's something quite wrong. These practices are insisting that we can produce pleasure with very odd things, very strange parts of our bodies, in very unusual situations. (Gallagher and Wilson, 1984, pp. 27-8)

Furthermore, given the fluid nature of roles for the S/M participants and the sense of a strategic game at work, Foucault (Gallagher and Wilson, 1984) sees S/M as a way to make ironic institutional power by eroticizing the relations that constitute it:

> This strategic game as a source of bodily pleasure is very interesting. But I wouldn't say that it is a reproduction, inside the erotic relationship, of the structure of power. It is an acting out of power structures by a strategic game that is able to give sexual pleasure. . . and is the creation of pleasure, and there is an identity in that creation. (Gallagher and Wilson, 1984, p. 30)

Gay sexual experiences create new spaces for relationships by transferring the social into the sexual arena, and making the social over into something new, something erotic. That, for Foucault, more than simply the legalization of gay rights, is the real possibility contemporary gay politics opens up in his understanding of the history of sexuality. And ultimately the power of this movement and its politics of difference lies in its ability to represent and reconstitute the body, desire, and sexuality as diverse through a critique of institutional power.

Chapter 3

Contemporary Cultural Analysis of Constructions of Gay Identity in Representations of AIDS

Against the backdrop of the history of sexuality in general and the particular history of gay and lesbian liberation, and the backlash against such a sexual movement, this discussion turns now to the issue of AIDS and gay identity in the 1980s. This chapter first examines the nature of mainstream representations of AIDS and gays in medical, media, and governmental discourse that sought to remedicalize homosexuality, both through communication that presented itself as educative and informational, and through silence. In fact, such communication has had the consequence of associating, in an essential way, representations of disease, otherness, and annihilation with gay identity.

The second part of this chapter explores the responses of the gay communities to such representations and associations. Such communication, for and by gays and lesbians, became more than ever organized around fervent efforts to critique mainstream representations of gay sexualities as diseased. Such alternative communication sought to reconstruct a gay voice that was powerful and resistant to institutional discourse.

I argue that two points merit particular attention here as seminal for communication about gay identity in the 1980s. First, communication by and for marginal communities again is organized around acts of reverse discourse, in which that which is labeled as diseased and deadly is represented as human, power-ful, and politically cogent; gay politics prior to the 1980s pro-vided such a precedent. Second, gay responses to mainstream representations relied heavily on communicating about gay sexu-ality and safe sex in erotic and sex-positive ways. This has been especially important for a marginal group that has been defined by and organized around sexual liberation. Very literally, the gay community's eroticization of safe sex has allowed for the mar-ginal group's continued subjectivity in the face of attempts to render it abject and nonexistent.

MAINSTREAM REPRESENTATIONS OF AIDS AND GAYS

The most prolific work dealing with AIDS and the social construction of gay identity in the 1980s has focused on the rhetoric of mainstream media representations. Crimp (1988a) in fact says that AIDS must be understood essentially as a disease of representation, and it is through this recognition that people can gain control over it:

> AIDS does not exist apart from the practices that conceptu-alize it, represent it, and respond to it. We know AIDS only in and through those practices. This assertion does not con-test the existence of viruses, antibodies, infections, or trans-mission routes. Least of all does it contest the reality of illness, suffering, and death. What it does contest is the notion that there is an underlying reality of AIDS, upon which are constructed the representations, or the culture, or the politics of AIDS. If we recognize that AIDS exists only in and through these constructions, then hopefully we can also recognize the imperative to know them, analyze them, and wrest control of them. (Crimp, 1988a, p. 3)

Thus, to recognize AIDS as a disease of representation is to politicize and demythologize AIDS.

Weeks (1989b) offers a historical overview of the progress of the disease during the 1980s that also serves as a framework for understanding the nature of mainstream representations (also see Altman, 1986). From 1981-1982, three major issues emerged: anxiety of the affected and discourse about safe sex and the politics of the medical community; the early medical definition and control of AIDS; and the governmental response of indifference. During 1982-1985, representations of AIDS and gays reflected, expressed, and constituted a moral panic: "the marginality of the PWA [person with AIDS], and its [AIDS's] identification as a 'gay plague,' were central to the second phase" (Weeks, 1989b, pp. 4-5). During this phase, AIDS also became a "potential symbolic agent" as the media, science, and government associated the disease with homosexual lifestyles; also, during this period, there emerged the gay and lesbian self-help response in the form of safe sex education as prevention. In 1985, with the much publicized death of Rock Hudson, the government began to respond with a public health campaign aimed at prevention of the spread of the virus; this has ultimately led to the professionalization of an organized response to AIDS in terms of both education and representation (Weeks, 1989b). The above offers a framework for discussing the structure and central themes that constitute mainstream representations of AIDS throughout the 1980s.

How do these representations work culturally? Watney (1987a), one of the most prolific scholars on the rhetoric of AIDS*, argues that mainstream discourse relies on associations between homosexuality and forbidden desire:

> as if the syndrome were a direct function of a particular sexual act—sodomy—and, by extension, of homosexual desire in all its forms . . . the entire discourse of AIDS turns

---

*See also Watney, 1988a,b; 1989a,b; 1990.

round the rhetorical figure of "promiscuity," as if all non-gays were either monogamous or celibate and, more culpably still, as if AIDS were related to sex in a quantitative rather than qualitative way . . . promiscuity . . . is being employed to other purposes—as a sign of homosexuality itself, of forbidden pleasures, of threat. (Watney, 1987a, p. 12)

Watney (1987) sees this identification of the homosexual with forbidden pleasure and desire as organized around the culture's anxiety about identity. The culture privileges and creates a desire for a singular, fixed identity; this desire carries with it the consequence of a fear of diversity, particularly sexual diversity. The homosexual, according to Watney (1987a), presents the most unsettling position for the heterosexual because "the gay man is truly polymorphous: he may fuck and be fucked" (Watney, 1987a, p. 28). This polymorphous identity runs counter to and strikes at the heart of mainstream media representations of sexuality, which always privilege a fixed identity as superior, as something to be desired.

Because of the homosexual's existential positioning as infectious other in the culture, institutions such as the media are able to construct representations of AIDS and gays around the following: gays are guilty victims of the disease; gays are infectious and the cause of the disease; gay desire and sexuality (whatever those might be) are themselves essentially diseased. As an illustration of how such representational constructions work, Watney (1987) offers a politicization of the conflation of HIV and AIDS common to media representations: "the political and social consequences of this woeful conflation of the virus (HIV) and AIDS become apparent in the slippage into the rhetoric of 'AIDS carriers' and the 'AIDS test.' Talk of 'AIDS carriers' establishes a discourse that brings the entire cultural legacy of contagion and 'plague' into operation. It implies that people with

AIDS are themselves threatening to the rest of the population, rather than threatened—clinically and socially" (Watney, 1987b, p. 50). Ultimately, Watney sees the media as being as heterosexualized as the representations they offer. The media name a general public and constitute a moral panic about anything that exists outside of the collective fantasy that supports and defends ideologically the heterosexual family. All else is perverse and abject.

Regarding the press and television specifically, Watney (1987a) identifies a series of visual strategies in press and television stories that work to stigmatize the homosexual under the guise of educating the general public about AIDS, a guise that effectively communicates disinformation about both AIDS and gays. First, the press and television discuss AIDS in terms of the future and the possibility that it will spread to heterosexuals and wipe all off the face of the earth; this precludes, according to Watney, a grounding of AIDS in the present and an examination of the hundreds of thousands of gays who have died and are dying from the syndrome. Second, the media link AIDS with large numbers of sexual encounters, rather than the quality of sexual encounters; this constructs homosexuality as promiscuous and antifamilial, establishes guilty and innocent victims, and ultimately relies on calls for quarantining the guilty—gay men—in order to protect the innocent—the heterosexual general public. And this last point, of course, is the most disturbing, because narratively it calls for violence to be carried out on the body of the gay man in order to preserve the heterosexual family and the social order; as Watney (1989a) concludes, "AIDS commentary suggests that . . . large sections of the population are calmly and routinely regarded in their entirety as disposable constituencies" (p. 69).

In order to resist the normalizing effect of mainstream discourse, which constructs AIDS as a justifiable, gay disease, the discourse must be read as the political construct it is, one that makes use of and constitutes sexuality as a means of maintaining existing power relationships and methods of surveillance. In an attempt to resist mainstream discourse, the theorists discussed below examine the specific discursive strategies used in AIDS representations–strategies that remain intact throughout the 1980s–that attempt to naturalize the association between gay identity and disease.

Several "resistant" theorists have focused on the linguistic construction of the disease given the above context. Grover (1988) focuses on the linguistic nature of AIDS by identifying words and terms often used incorrectly by the media, politicians, and scientists: for example, "AIDS carrier," "AIDS victim," "homosexual," "risk group," and "the AIDS test" all work to position gays medically in a way that associates them as a group with the disease itself. Grover (1988) concludes that "such a critical attention to language is essential to our understanding of and response to AIDS as the cultural construction that it is. AIDS is not simply a physical malady; it is also an artifact of social and sexual transgression, violated taboo, fractured identity–political and personal projections" (p. 18). By focusing on the political consequences for gays of mainstream media word choice, Grover dislodges discourse used in the construction of AIDS and gays from what is often a seemingly objective position provided by media and other institutions.

Treichler (1988) likewise concurs that AIDS must be examined at the level of language in order to understand it for what it is: "the name AIDS in part constructs the disease and helps make it intelligible. We cannot therefore look 'through' language to determine what AIDS 'really is.' Rather we must explore the site where such determinations really occur and intervene at the point where meaning is created: in language" (p. 31). Treichler uses this foundation in language to discuss how scientists in the early days of the disease linked AIDS to and defined gay lifestyles and sexual practices, constructed the disease in terms of contagions, and claimed the cause to be a single agent, language that, given the source, constituted homophobia as scientific, objective truth. As this scientific discourse becomes the focus of much mainstream media coverage of AIDS (McAllister, 1992), homophobia is further institutionalized.

Such homophobic constructions work in part because of the binary oppositions on which they rely. Landers (1988) examines how these oppositions are used in commercial television representations. Like Watney, he sees commercial television as positing a heterosexual reality; he also concurs that programming on AIDS "suggests that gays exist outside and against this 'reality,' their deaths bearing little consequence" (Landers, 1988, p. 19). However, Landers extends Watney's discussion/deconstruction by examining ways mainstream representations focus on the body of the homosexual. To interpret how these representations work, Landers identifies the following binary oppositions used in commercial discussions of AIDS: body–straight, healthy, innocent; anti-body–gay, diseased, guilty (McGrath, 1990). Through these positionings, homosexual desire is linked with disease, and the homosexual is seen as doomed, the undead (Hanson, 1991; Nunokawa, 1991); furthermore, like illness, homosexuality becomes something that can be cured with self-control and discipline, which buys into "new right thinking . . . that stresses individualism while concealing an agenda of state intervention, control, and surveillance of morality" (Landers, 1988, p. 21). Landers ultimately historicizes this construction of the homosexual body with the evolution of the photograph into an agent used by the middle class and medical communities to document, create, and fix aberrant persons. Landers calls this a politics of visibility, a strategy used to survey, control, discipline, and constitute the homosexual as deviant and diseased.

The above binary oppositions work in representations about AIDS because they allow mainstream audiences to discursively block themselves from AIDS and gay desire; homosexuality, like illness, comes to be seen as something that is alien to mainstream audiences. Gilman (1988) describes this culture's historical representation of disease and illness as work done to mark the "other" with invisibility or monstrosity and, thereby, mark all else as different from the other, which, for dominant culture, solidifies a whole and coherent self rather than a fragmented one. It is through fragmentation from the position of other that people are able to maintain "proof that we are still whole, healthy, and sane; and that we are not different, diseased, or mad" (Gilman, 1988, pp. 271-2).

Narrative strategies also work to constitute the "other" in mainstream communication about AIDS. Williamson (1989) examines AIDS representations that are organized around horror, melodrama, and detective narratives in which the audience looks to specialists—medical, scientific, and governmental experts—to effectively uncover a threat—gay desire and identity—and the specialist unravels and solves the mystery (p. 72). Seidman (1988) further identifies narrative strategies that work to place homosexuals in the position of "other" and insert them into a "drama of pollution and purity" (p. 189) in which gays pollute the purity of heterosexuality.

Singer (1993) identifies a discursive strategy in much mainstream communication about AIDS that she calls "epidemic logic" which draws on and extends the above analysis of media discourse. She argues that such discourse constructs excessive representations of the disease and associations with gays that evoke an extreme response of surveillance as a way of controlling the epidemic. The surveillance response is not only justified by the text, but incited by it.

By examining the cultural context, linguistic maneuvers, narrative structures, and binary systems of meaning, the above theorists are able to resist mainstream discourse about AIDS. To accomplish such a politicized reading, they, like Foucault, look archaeologically at the structures of discourse that constitute identity for gays in AIDS representations, and they insist on the cultural construction of and link between recent and historical, especially nineteenth century, representations. This genealogical politicization embodies the very tenets of Foucault's analysis of power, language, and identity.

In an edited collection of essays called *Ecstatic Antibodies,* Marshall (1990) makes explicit a Foucauldian reading of the history of representations of gays and AIDS that builds upon and synthesizes the above theorists. He claims that in mainstream, dominant representations, "gay men are . . . troubled by a dearth, a poverty, a starvation diet of representation" (Marshall, 1990, p. 20). But recently, with AIDS, images of gays have proliferated in television and the press, and gays are linked with degenerative death, and this "reworks a pathology" already in place (Marshall, 1990, p. 22).

Marshall (1990) offers an example of this pathology in medical discourse and representation in Bedlam during the nineteenth century and the evolution and use of photography: "the task of documenting the physiognomy of deviant types . . . was greatly facilitated by the invention of photography" (p. 24). Marshall connects the creation of the homosexual with the advent of photography by claiming that this is an example of new ways that institutions sought to manage and create information (also see Gilman, 1988). This management is tied to medical discourse, which enabled the state to survive and control populations through the science of sexology and the medicalization of sexuality and deviancy. The photograph enables the gaze of the medical profession and the state by making the homosexual and the deviant visible, embodied. This condition of surveillance vigorously recurs in the 1980s with mainstream representations of gays in conjunction with AIDS.

Marshall and the above analysts link linguistic and imagistic representations of AIDS and gays to a cultural and historical context that gives rise both to the control of the homosexual and to the existence of the homosexual. In a move of reverse discourse, however, gays and lesbians in the 1980s have responded to these representations by solidifying and creating new opportunities for survival.

QUEER RESPONSES TO MAINSTREAM REPRESENTATIONS

Meyer (1993) understands the photography of Robert Mapplethorpe as a radical response to the traditional objectification of the camera's subject; his human subjects, often participants in gay sadomasochism, stare defiantly at the camera, in control of their own image. In Mapplethorpe's 1988 self-portrait, taken while he was living with AIDS, he too stares defiantly at the camera as his hand grasps a cane with a skeleton's head for a tip. Meyer (1993) reads this photograph in a way that synthesizes the gay and lesbian communities' responses to their representations in media, science, government discourse–defined as education about AIDS:

> It [the self-portrait] explicitly refutes the economy of concerned or "victim" in the face of cultural fear. Through its very theatricality (white fist grasping death's-head cane in near space, white face floating in deeper space, all set within a monochrome of black), the *Self-Portrait* asserts Mapplethorpe's authority over his self-representation. While the visual repercussions of AIDS are there to be seen in the face of Robert Mapplethorpe, the very force of his photographic abstraction contests the patheticizing operations of victim photography . . . in this image . . . Mapplethorpe meets and then defies the gaze of his own camera. In so doing, he signals the radical insufficiency of photography to describe the experiences, and here the vulnerabilities, of his sentient body. (Meyer, 1993, pp. 376-7)

Mapplethorpe employs photography to reassert his power over, and in the face of, AIDS. Given Meyer's reading, Mapplethorpe's use of photography can be said to be engaging in Foucault's concept of reverse discourse in which one who is the object of surveillance via discourse reverses, or deconstructs, the discourse in order to enter as an active and ironic subject of that discourse. And this is largely how gays have responded to their own representations in messages about AIDS.

The earliest responses by gays came from grassroots organizations in large urban areas that formed to combat what they saw as the desexualization, remedicalization, and annihilation of gay identity in the early 1980s. Indeed, the most political responses from gay and lesbian communities have come in the form of safe sex education, care for PLWAs, and in "your" face activism.

Two of the earliest and most successful efforts to reverse mainstream discourse used to talk about gays and AIDS came from the San Francisco AIDS Foundation (SFAF) in California and Gay Men's Health Crisis (GMHC) in New York. According to Kayal (1993), in *Bearing Witness: Gay Men's Health Crisis and the Politics of AIDS*, GMHC was formed by a group of influential gay men in the summer of 1981 (the year *The New York Times* reported the first story of a new gay cancer that had afflicted 41 homosexuals on the East and West coasts, in the apartment of the playwright) Larry Kramer, who later formed ACT UP (AIDS Coalition To Unleash Power). This group of volunteers raised money, started an educational effort, and began to offer care to People Living With AIDS (PLWAs) and People with AIDS-Related Complex (PARCs). In 1983, GMHC became incorporated and currently operates with a $20 million annual budget and an active volunteer staff of over 2,000 (Kayal, 1993, p. 2). GMHC not only offers social support services to New Yorkers afflicted with AIDS, it, along with the SFAF offers educational materials to federal and state agencies throughout the United States. Kayal (1993) uses GMHC as an example of the kind of volunteer-based, grass roots organizations that gays formed in the 1980s to foster a sense of community ownership of AIDS prevention and treatment and gay responsibility for PLWA care. This emphasis on grass roots organizing and the formation of collectives is crucial to coalescing gay power in the early stages of the epidemic, and it also becomes definitional for gay politics throughout the decade, as an emphasis comes to be placed on coalition building with other minorities within and outside of gay communities.

One of GMHC's main goals has always been to provide realistic education to gays that emphasizes safe, erotic sex. For example, in 1985, Palacios-Jimenez and Shernoff, two early GMHC volunteers, put together a workshop to teach people how to eroticize safe sex; GMHC published this educational tract in 1986 and 1989, and today it remains one of the most cutting-edge approaches to safe and erotic sex education for gay men in this country (Palacios-Jimenez and Shernoff, 1989).

Why is the eroticization of safe sex in AIDS and HIV prevention education for gay men so important and how can it be achieved? Watney (1987a) sees sexuality for gay men traversing a wide range of social and interpersonal possibilities: "for most gay men, sex involves a far broader degree of general eroticized physical contact, in which fucking and sucking are episodes of intimacy among others . . . gay sex is about maximizing the mutual erotic possibilities of the body" (p. 127). He argues that one of the ways to make safe sex acceptable is to understand it in the framework of the erotic, which is central to gay sexualities. Education can accomplish this, Watney claims, by mobilizing fantasy:

> What we need to establish is a sex education campaign aimed at gay men in the form of "compromise-formations," which would permit what is understood as the loss of certain sexual pleasures to be sublimated in relation to gains at the level of fantasy . . . we urgently need to enlarge and

expand our sense of the sexual, in order to incorporate condoms as new stage props into the theater of our desiring
fantasies. (Watney, 1987a, p. 133)

Crimp (1988b), in fact, argues that it is gay men's love of sex
that has allowed them to respond to AIDS successfully; they are
able to rethink sexuality because they are not averse to talking
about it. "Promiscuous" views of sex are also able to deal with
the subject of safe sex pluralistically and creatively.

Patton (1990a) sees gay community-based educative and representational efforts regarding erotic safe sex, especially prior to 1986
and the "heterosexual AIDS scare," as working against traditional,
highly conservative, public health campaigns in which the government "imparted knowledge" by "valorizing the innocent and de-
monizing the guilty" (p. 7). Public health campaigns usually present governmental positions as objective information/knowledge/
truth to audiences, dismissing identities/communities not in line
with the "general populace." The early response of gay activists to
mainstream representations of AIDS and themselves is an example
of a community refusing to accept disciplinary and discursive re-
legation of homosexuality to a position of sex-negativity.

In general, gay community-based erotic safe sex education,
such as that produced by national organizations such as GMHC
and SFAF and by local organizations, visually depict men, and
more recently women, involved in various sexually explicit activities in which condoms or other latex devices are used; textually, explicit language is also employed to define exactly what safe
sex is, how it is enacted, and how it can be erotic. These messages cater to different subpopulations within the gay communities, such as leather and cowboy, and are designed around various sexual activities, such as mutual and group masturbation,
oral or anal sex, sadomasochism, water sports, and phone sex.
Gay communities thereby construct erotic messages that speak to

their desires and correspond to their various relationships to the world.

Patton (1991) offers a more exact and theoretically compelling explanation of safe sex messages. In an essay about safe sex representations in gay pornography, she discusses her attempt to create a safe sex video that is "hot and liberatory," thereby broadening what can be constituted as safe sex. In order to achieve this, she must first decide what exactly constitutes, and has constituted, the representation of safe sex. She concludes that safe sex must be shown realistically and fully; the written text and sexual practices must entail more than condom use, which cannot be seen as dull; and issues of gay male sexuality must be dealt with using a variety of sexual strategies and in a way that broadens the creation of a safe sex environment (Patton, 1991, p. 36). These features are common to community-based messages.

What is particularly interesting about safe sex educational campaigns during these early years is the way they play out Foucault's hypothesis, discussed earlier, about what contemporary gay politics have to offer. Not only does the gay response resist and deconstruct the remedicalization of homosexuality, it does so by playing on diverse and multiple relational experiences and positions people take with themselves and others. These relationships, like safe sex education by and for gays, often perform the act of deconstruction through the eroticization of power relationships, and the celebration of the unstable nature of sexual positioning.

THE PROFESSIONALIZATION OF SAFE SEX

As mentioned earlier, a shift in AIDS discourse occurs in 1985 with the highly publicized and visible death, and outing, of actor Rock Hudson. At this point, the government began its attempt to gain control of AIDS education by adopting safe sex education and disseminating a sterile and institutionally funded version of the messages gay activists created in the early years of the disease. Patton (1990b) identifies at least two important concerns for gays during this period: testing becomes linked with education; and public health education becomes bifurcated into campaigns that target the "general population" and those designed for "communities at risk."

According to Patton (1990b), these two factors institutionally reinforce the antigay information campaigns of the early 1980s. First, testing, besides reintroducing the possibility for policing and quarantining homosexuals, reinforces the notion of risk groups rather than risk behaviors, and provides people with disinformation about safe sex:

> The mere idea of a test—regardless of what it actually detects, and regardless of its reliability and validity—means that individuals could know their status, and that a policing public health system could find it out. This displaces all responsibility for "safety" onto the putatively or provable HIV seropositive person and implies that there could be no such thing as consent to unsafe sex with a seropositive person . . . by confusing the relationship between safe sex (as a set of acts) and sero-status (as a determinant of the possibility of infection) promoted by test-backed education, many people have difficulty associating transmission promoting acts with the people they love and trust. (Patton, 1990b, p. 100)

Such confusion about safe sex as an act to be performed depending upon whom one is having sex with, instead of an integral part of all sexual experiences, reveals the very danger posed by public health campaigns that continue to stigmatize gay communities.

Additionally, Patton argues that the government's bifurcation of public health campaigns into public and community-based approaches inaccurately relieves people whose activities put them at risk (which is basically everyone) of the obligation to be educated about and practice safe sex:

> The public was no longer those who had managed to keep AIDS at a distance and became instead, those people "not at risk." "Risk group" terminology broke down under protest from the minority communities, who soon discovered that the once-empowering word "community" would now be equated with "risk group." The new messages . . . changed the question for the individual from "how do I avoid this virus?" to "which of these 'you's' am I?" The selection of information now depended on an individual's perception of membership in either the public or a community, a change in nomenclature which retained the confusion between difference and risk. (Patton, 1990b, p. 101)

Furthermore, within the context of a bifurcated audience, public health campaigns operate on the following assumption about the responsibility for knowledge: "even though each group received 'facts,' the public is given information on the assumption that they have a right to know, that is, a right to 'protect' themselves, while 'communities' are educated on the assumption that they have an obligation to know and protect the 'public'" (Patton, 1990b, p. 103). Patton claims that high rates of transmission will continue as long as scientific discourse continues in public health campaigns that reinforces people as responsible for AIDS and not certain unprotected sexual activities that all people participate in, regardless of orientation affiliation and identity:

> Science, or rather, the governance of the political by scientific discourse, equals death for people living with HIV. Silence, or rather, educators' failure to speak for fear of inciting the body to acts of pleasure that are now defined as 'risks,' prevents specific classes of people from obtaining information—about safe sex and needle hygiene—that will

save their lives. And this can only be described as death by disinformation. (Patton, 1990b, p. 131)

In spite of the emphasis on testing and the bifurcation of messages that the institutionalization of AIDS education enacted, much community-based safe sex education continues to be erotic and sex positive after 1985. However, the government's funding of such messages came under scrutiny with the passage of the 1988 Helms amendment to the Senate's AIDS education, treatment, and research bill; the amendment prohibited federal funds from being used to produce and disseminate information about explicit homosexual activity. State health departments, an example of which is given in Chapter 5, have dealt with this restriction by contracting work out to local community organizations that can create this information for the state; the health departments then disseminate the information, which does not carry the department's name and can therefore be funded with federal dollars.

What becomes crucial as AIDS activism, and the disease itself, moves into the 1990s is that the language used in safe sex messages must become more sensitive to the needs of minority groups, such as people of color, women, and IV drug users, within gay communities. To return to Patton's (1991) discussion of safe sex representations in gay porn, she claims that erotic, safe, and liberatory sex has been discursively realized only through the linguistic vernacular of upper- or middle-class white gay men. And, indeed, safe sex campaigns at the community level are often organized around language that speaks primarily to white gay male populations. Patton (1991) explains the problem as follows: current erotic community-based safe sex messages, regardless of whom within gay and lesbian communities they are designed for, treat sexual explicitness in the language of privileged, upwardly mobile gay white men, and this is seen as natural, as the only meaning of sexual explicitness. Language in these representations is thus treated unproblematically, and "equates specific acts with corresponding, technically correct words" (Patton, 1991, p. 40). The consequence is that the "language of the marginal becomes redefined in terms of dominant culture . . . appropriation robs the vernacular of its linguistic polysemy and temporal specificity . . . and linguistic transgression is equated with realism" (Patton, 1991, pp. 41-3). Recent activist education reaches out to a much broader range of minority communities and is encouraging their participation in the construction and dissemination of safe sex messages that will privilege more diverse vernaculars and systems of meaning. In this context, what remains important about AIDS education is that "HIV/AIDS education must always be political. HIV/AIDS education either reinscribes the sexual, class, and racial ideologies that are propped up by moralism and science, or disrupts the hierarchical formation of knowledge and opens up space for groups and communities to work out their interrelationships with information they have decided is relevant" (Patton, 1990b, p. 105). Effective safe sex education, consequently, will work to encourage and empower the voices of multiple marginal communities who are being affected by the disease.

EDUCATION AS ACTIVISM

Reacting, in more traditionally political ways, to the governmental, scientific, and medical communities' response to AIDS and HIV by the mid-1980s, gays in 1987 formed the political group ACT UP, which sought to make visible the criminal actions that were being directed against gays. This can be read as a significant shift in, or addition to, gay and AIDS activism in the 1980s as education came to include radical acts of civil disobedience aimed at directing the blame for AIDS at the government; AIDS education thus becomes overtly and essentially a political experience. Most interesting, given the culture's attempts to police gays by making them visible, is ACT UP's focus on tactics and strategies of representation.

In *AIDS Demographics,* Crimp and Rolston (1990), early members of ACT UP New York, the original ACT UP group, reflect this emphasis on representation not only in discussion of ACT UP but in the purpose of the book itself: "this book is intended as a demonstration, in both senses of the word. It is meant as direct action, putting the power of representation in the hands of as many people as possible" (p. 13). One of ACT UP's most interesting, postmodern approaches to the politics and construction of representations is the appropriation of images from different contexts to create a new context that privileges the disenfranchised perspective:

> Part of our point is that nobody owns these images. They belong to a movement that is constantly growing—in numbers, in militancy, in political awareness . . . questions of identity, authorship, and audience—and the ways in which all three are constructed through representation—have been central to postmodern art, theory, and criticism. The significance of so-called appropriation art, in which the artist forgoes the claim to original creation by appropriating already existing images and objects, has been to show that the unique individual is a kind of fiction, that our very selves are socially and historically determined through pre-existing images, discourses and events. (Crimp and Rolston, 1990, pp. 15 and 18).

So ACT UP's vision and politics are not just a re-visioning of historical and cultural contexts, they are a reconstruction of identity; and again, long after Foucault's death, a playing-out can be observed of his understanding of the contribution of contemporary gay politics to possibilities for alternative relationships to oneself and others. Indeed, Crimp and Rolston's (1990) description of ACT UP's representations goes to the heart of gay activ-

ism during the 1980s: "our graphics played a Foucauldian twist
. . . turning the confession of sexual identity into a declaration of
sexual politics: I am out, therefore I am" (p. 102).

In the early years of the group, ACT UP engaged in numerous
acts of civil disobedience directed at the Reagan administration and
garnered national media attention; in fact, one of the group's most
successful techniques was its ability to create media events and use
mainstream media to make visible the plight of gays and lesbians in
the wake of AIDS and governmental inaction. Some of ACT UP's
more famous protests were the 1987 march on Wall Street and the
1988 shutdown of the Food and Drug Administration (Crimp and
Rolston, 1990).

Finally, as famous as are these demonstrations, as Crimp and
Rolston mention above, is ACT UP's creation and use of activist
art, especially the inverted pink triangle on a black background
with the slogan "Silence = Death;" this is one of the most striking and significant political symbols of gay activism in recent
times. Crimp and Rolston (1990) explains the significance:

> That simple graphic emblem . . . has come to signify AIDS
> activism to an entire community of people confronting the
> epidemic. This in itself tells us something about the styles
> and strategies of the movement's graphics. For "Silence =
> Death" does its work with a metaphorical subtlety that is
> unique, among political symbols and slogans, to AIDS ac-
> tivism. Our emblem's significance depends on foreknowl-
> edge of the use of the pink triangle as the marker of gay men
> in Nazi concentration camps, its appropriation by the gay
> movement to remember a suppressed history of our oppres-
> sion, and, now, an inversion of its positioning (men in the
> death camps wore triangles that pointed down; Silence =
> Death's points up). Silence = Death declares that silence
> about the oppression and annihilation of gay people, then
> and now, must be broken as a matter of our survival. As

historically problematic as an analogy of AIDS and the death camps is, it is also deeply resonant for gay men and lesbians, especially insofar as the analogy is already mediated by the gay movement's adoption of the pink triangle. (Crimp and Rolston, 1990, p. 14)

Not everyone agrees that the symbol is positive and life-affirming. Marshall (1991), for instance, is disturbed by the use of the Nazi death camp symbol since it invites comparison to Hitler's genocide of Jews.

No real parallel can be drawn between the extermination of Jews in the Final Solution and the extermination of homosexuals. The extermination of Jews was conceived by the Nazis precisely as the extermination of a 'race,' which unless sterilized and gassed would continue to propagate its putative racial characteristics. The problem with homosexuals, as far as the Third Reich was concerned, was the fact that they supposedly did not reproduce. (Marshall, 1991, p. 77)

Moreover, Marshall notes that silence equaled life in Nazi Germany, as denial of homosexuality kept many from being sent to their deaths. He argues for a less victimized symbol and for multiple symbols that celebrate difference and diversity within gay and lesbian communities.

Edelman (1989) offers a deconstructive reading of the slogan "Silence = Death" and concludes that it relies on and reinforces a binary opposition and, therefore, treats the literal as a metaphor, undermining the ideological point that gay people's bodies are being destroyed by AIDS because of the government.

However, Crimp (1989) claims that it is precisely because of the symbol's metaphoric possibilities and slippage that it can stand for a broad range of suffering and militancy in gay and lesbian communities. The very fact of the symbol's slippage and disjuncture from traditional stories of histories of victims, and its figural ability to stand for more than the literal, emerges as the power of the symbol. And again the way this symbol works connects with Foucault and his analysis of gay relationships and politics based on reverse discourse.

In conclusion, gay and lesbian communities have responded and are responding deconstructively through discourses of education and activism to mainstream representations of same sex desire, disease, and homosexuality. In the following chapter, examples of two different kinds of messages and representations will be examined in light of the above contextualization of the decade that sought to remedicalize gay desires. What becomes clear from these examples, which arise after the government's professionalization and institutionalization of safe sex education, is the continuing effort of the state to constitute all desire as something that must be policed and kept under surveillance through communication about public health. However, also continuing is the effort by communities to insist on their presence through the celebration of sexual diversity.

Chapter 4

The Cultural Construction
of the General Public
in a National Public Service
Announcement Health Campaign

I deploy the analysis synthesized to this point to examine a national public service announcement campaign designed for the "general public." I argue that these public health messages appear to offer general health information about HIV and AIDS prevention without political perspective; however, by employing an analysis of the discursive ways sexuality, identity, and power are constructed and communicated, I show that these messages support an agenda that stigmatizes gays, despite the fact that they are presented as scientific, informational, and value-free.

This discussion focuses on a national public service announcement (PSA) campaign designed for, and that constructs, what is often called the "general public" or, in the case of AIDS messages, nongay persons; as such, this example attempts to effectively silence, thus stigmatize, the marginal voice and ultimately treat it as abject, the humanly unrepresentable.

The analysis that follows will not attempt to empirically or

A preliminary discussion of the initial findings of this study was presented in the following form:

Myrick, R., Trivoulidis, N., Swanson, D., Lam, K., and Al-Qhtani, S. (1992). "Representation of AIDS in Televised Public Service Announcements: The Discursive Practices of Government in the Constitution of Knowledge About AIDS." Paper presented at the annual meeting of the Speech Communication Association, Chicago.

quantitively prove the producer's intent or the effect the PSAs have on an audience. Instead, the analysis of the PSAs will attempt to understand one possible way these messages make sense given the historical and political context discussed in Chapters 1, 2, and 3. More specifically, this chapter will look at the ways these messages participate in strategies of meaning that silence the gay voice and simultaneously encourage its proliferation. In both cases, the discourse works to control identity through communication.

FOUCAULDIAN APPROACH TO ANALYSIS OF PSAs

What becomes important in mass media messages about AIDS, in light of the rhetorical maneuvers discussed in Chapter 3, are the kinds of subjectivities that are being constructed in the public health messages and the kinds of perspectives, or truths, that are being endorsed. One of the key concerns here will be the construction of the "general public" and marginal groups and what can be known about them. Ultimately, AIDS PSAs construct and treat what is known as the "general public" as a fixed and unproblematic entity, one that is represented as a majority voice, and the marginal remains unrepresented, at least in human form, in the messages.

How does the "general public" come to be represented as unproblematically normal in these communicative acts? The PSAs accomplish such a normalization by treating knowledge, truth, and subjectivity in public health messages as fixed, existing independently of the message, and thus reinforce a seemingly unproblematic account of AIDS, the "general public," and gay identity. The result is a mystification of the production of what can be taken as subjectivity and knowledge; ultimately the messages appear depoliticized and innocuously uninformative. Assumptions about the production of meaning go unquestioned, and this reifies existing power relationships that define the nature of knowledge in the PSAs under consideration.

Using a Foucauldian analysis of the PSA messages at the level of discourse allows for an examination of the constitutive power of language in the creation and representation of subjects and knowledge–and focuses on the power relationships at work that constitute meaning. This approach, which directly mirrors Shapiro's (1984) deployment of Foucault discussed earlier, allows for the demystification of subjects and knowledge–showing them for the linguistic and political constructions they are, a particularly important position for an analysis of the marginal voice in PSAs. This approach thus acts to politicize the message by analyzing the way the text produces and expresses meaning; in the context of Chapter 3, this meaning can ultimately be understood as a construction of the marginal as threatening and heterosexual families as biologically normal.

TEXTUAL ANALYSIS OF PSAs

The PSAs selected for analysis are recent attempts by the U.S. Department of Health and Human Services (HHS) to address, and thus construct, the general public and a teenage audience–a group that is currently one of the segments most rapidly being infected by the HIV virus. The HHS oversees the Centers for Disease Control (CDC) which is charged with the responsibility of creating and producing educational materials for the "general public"; the CDC then distributes these materials to state and local departments of health, media outlets, and various educational groups. At the state and local departments of health, media outlets, and various educational groups. At the state and local level, health departments decide which materials are appropriated for dissemination to the public.

The PSAs analyzed come from the HHS's 1991 educational series and include one state-produced PSA. Representative examples from this series are summarized and discussed below; written transcripts of the PSAs appear in appendixes. For the purposes of organization, the PSAs are classified into two categories according to communication strategies and the organizations identified with the messages. The first PSAs discussed are textually identified with the Ad Council, the National Institute of Drug Abuse, and the U.S. Department of Health and Human Services; this group of PSAs will subsequently be referred to as the Ad Council set. The second group of PSAs examined are textually identified with the CDC's national educational campaign, "America Responds to AIDS"; this group will be referred to as the CDC set.

While interesting differences between the two sets are noted, the HHS is ultimately responsible for the politics of the discursive strategies used in all of the PSAs, and, substantively and politically, the two sets are indistinguishable. The focus of the analysis here is the consequence of the discursive practices in the PSAs that create subjects and meaning through various representational strategies.

In the PSAs from the Ad Council, the general message communicated is that AIDS is deadly, that it comes from being irresponsible with drugs, and that it affects heterosexual teenagers. The Ad Council uses a very stylized, MTV-esque production approach, one that foregrounds and juxtaposes postnuclear settings and heavy, foreboding colors.

What subjects do the discursive practices in the messages create? First, and most obviously, innocent subjects and potential innocent victims are heterosexualized, as only people engaging in heterosexual behavior are represented as human characters in the messages. The educative focus of each message is thus placed with the mainstream audience which is defined as heterosexual. The consequence of this focus is that it identifies people who can be saved from the disease as solely heterosexual; in fact, the only subjects that the audience should be concerned about are heterosexual, although the disease has not been discursively inflicted upon them as it has on gays. The ramifications of discursively privileging one particular sexual orientation and ignoring another, the homosexual, works to naturalize and legitimate heterosexuality. Knowledge about AIDS is the right of the heterosexual; s/he owns this knowledge. Conversely, the homosexual is visibly absent as a human character and is excluded from the right to this knowledge. So the message becomes, not one that addresses and educates teenagers or the public in general, but rather one that constitutes the relevant, *natural* subject as the subject who engages in activity defined as heterosexual. Although the homosexual is absent in terms of being represented as a human character in the PSA, s/he is actually quite present and constituted as a different kind of subject, a predatory, menacing, and ultimately justifiably infectious one.

The first PSA examined, "Ocean" (see Appendix A), opens with a slow pan and close-up shot of what appears to be a postnuclear beach, with layers of red, blue, and orange sewage advancing up the beach. The camera slowly pans up the bare stiff leg of a teenaged woman lying on the beach, and then pulls back to show the sewage ooze encroaching on the woman's leg. As the camera moves up the body of the woman, a young man moves onto the female, and they engage in an erotic interaction as the voice-over menacingly tells the listener that drugs can cloud judgment and enable one to forget about or disregard safe sex practices. The message states that this irresponsibility—in this case, responsibility for prevention rests with the woman—results in death. The message indicates that the couple on the beach are about to become infected by something unforeseen, something unrepresentable.

Beyond the heterosexuality of the innocent, soon-to-be-infected subjects, the PSA also represents the homosexual as subject in the message. However, the gay presence in the message is associated with and represented as the inhuman, sewage encroaching on and infecting the unsuspecting couple. This infectious, excremental image, as seen in Chapter 3, buys into cultural representations that associate homosexuality with passive anal sex, which ultimately threatens and deconstructs male power in the culture. Through this inhuman representation, the PSA constructs the homosexual as diseased, infectious, predatory, and, most important, anal; in light of the earlier discussion of mainstream representations of gays and AIDS, the message effectively conflates the homosexual and AIDS, and positions him/ it as the antithesis of what is healthy, normal, and life-affirming.

With the association of drug use and safe sex practices, the discourse also works to define AIDS, and thereby homosexuality, in the context of the federal government's "War on Drugs"– drugs being an established social problem during the Republican administrations of the 1980s. AIDS, and by implication homosexuality, as a subject then comes to be defined not primarily as a medical problem, but rather as a moral and social problem, like drugs. Thus AIDS as knowledge is defined as a punishment who falls on those members of the society who deviate from societal norms. The implication of defining AIDS as a social problem, rather than as a biological condition, is that the emphasis is placed on a condemnation of sexual diversity, rather than on the syndrome itself and the government's refusal to respond to the syndrome. This ultimately illustrates that AIDS is, for gays, a crisis of representation as much as it is a medical crisis, as discussed earlier by Crimp (1988a).

Moreover, the issue of responsibility is represented in a complex way, given these representations of innocent and infectious subjects. Knowledge about prevention of the disease is presented as the right of the heterosexual, while responsibility for the disease itself rests with the homosexual as he oozes up the beach to infect the heterosexual couple. The discourse thus not only defines what AIDS is, it also identifies the agents of power who should be concerned about and responsible for the prevention of the disease. The presence of the homosexual as the infectious ooze implies more than a simple sequestering of that voice; not only is the homosexual considered to be unimportant in terms of concern and preventative possibilities, but the identity culturally constructed as homosexual is depicted as essentially diseased and inhuman.

Essential to the above definition of AIDS and homosexuality as inhuman subject is the function of the postnuclear atmosphere. For example, when the ad begins, waves are splashing on the blue and red fluorescent beach; then, as the camera begins its slow pan, the waves recede, suggesting that life, associated with the ocean, can be recaptured only by heeding and complying with knowledge as defined by the discourse in the message. The alternative, death, lies in the red-blood- and excrement-covered sand on the beach, upon which rests the lifeless limb of a woman. In conjunction with this image, the music played is threatening, Wagnerian—suggesting impending doom, war, darkness. As the camera begins its pan, the narrator's voice seems to rise out of the threatening music. The narrator's tone is severe, authoritative, and, again, threatening, and his message is that AIDS will sneak up on and annihilate the couple on the beach and, ultimately, the audience.

This atmosphere textually synthesizes the various rhetorical features identified by the cultural theorists discussed in Chapter 3 concerning mainstream representations of AIDS and gays in messages presented as public health education. These elements include linguistic features that implicitly link homosexuality with disease and destruction; narrative structures that insert the homosexual into dramas of pollution, horror, and science fiction; and visual and imagistic representations of the homosexual body as essentially excremental. These rhetorical strategies work as systems of meaning because they play on cultural fears and anxieties about male power. Images of homosexuality linked with passive anal sex and excrement threaten this power, as Watney

(1989) claims, because they show the possibility of the masculine to be feminized, a position that is denied power in the culture.

In sum, a plurality of discursive practices are at work that succeed not simply in educating a mass audience, but in defining who that audience is, what counts as knowledge for that audience, and, ultimately, what relationship that audience has to itself and to those defined as others.

In the two remaining ads from the Ad Council, "Car" and "Roof" (see Appendixes B and C), the same discursive attempts are present that work to constitute subjectivity and reinforce the definitional power of the government/sponsor. One significant difference is worth noting: in the ad titled "Car," the agent responsible for prevention is identified as the male, while the female appears as the responsible agent in the other two ads. Interestingly, when the female is charged with the responsibility for prevention, the dominant images associated with the female are the elements of water and air; conversely, when the male is charged with responsibility, the dominant associative image is a car. Through the use of these metaphors to define male and female agency, the discourse again seems to naturalize and depoliticize power relationships and control and further reinscribe the biological normalcy of the binary opposition of masculinity and femininity, heterosexuality and homosexuality.

The other set of PSAs examined is identified with the CDC and its educational campaign, "America Responds to AIDS." In general, the same constitutions of subjects, power, and knowledge appear as those present in the Ad Council's ads. And, in fact, the PSAs that carry the Ad Council identification are produced, ultimately, by the HHS–via the CDC. However, several general differences in both approach and consequence are worth noting.

One striking difference between the ads from the two sources rests with the Ad Council's emphasis on visual technique to create an image of AIDS that is palatable as entertainment to a mass audience, particularly a heterosexual, teenaged one; safe sex messages are imagined as a commodity that can and should be consumed by the heterosexual audience, the "general public." In the CDC ads, the production techniques serve more as background for the people in the ads, the subjects. One consequence of this difference in production emphasis is that the CDC-sponsored ads seem to represent a more "realistic" look at AIDS, one that is more "natural" and, consequently, more legitimate than the postnuclear discourse of the Ad Council's messages. The messages and perspectives, and the construction of subjects and knowledges, appear even less politically charged than those in the Ad Council's PSAs.

A second difference can be identified with the positioning of the characters as narrators in the messages. The characters in the CDC ads are represented as controlling the narrative; there is no central, omniscient narrator as there is in the Ad Council ads. Instead, the characters are constituted as talking heads through the use of close-ups and familiar settings, interesting visually in terms of the positions of surveillance the heads seem to inhabit. These production techniques seem to empower those subjects, at least temporarily, with the ability and the discourse to talk about AIDS. The characters, in most cases, appear to be the holders of knowledge about the disease and its prevention. The talking heads speak directly to the audience, personalize the message, and emphasize a direct, informational approach to education, much more so than the dramatic, imagistic, and metaphoric approach to the subject seen in the Ad Council's ads.

However, in each of the PSAs identified with the CDC–and in all of the PSAs that were analyzed–talk about AIDS, which constitutes knowledge about AIDS, is reserved for the government's voice; specific information is available only by calling the government agency's toll free number, which is identified on the screen and presented by a narrator at the end of the message.

While it may seem that the characters as subjects are going to talk about AIDS, the ability to engage in discourse on this subject remains situated and organized around the government's discourse of itself as protector of a citizenship. The consequence is that the characters who seem to be constituted as subjects with knowledge are finally relegated to the position of passive objects until they engage in the government's discourse. This renders the government's voice as the most legitimate, powerful, unquestioned, and uncontested. Furthermore, while the audience seems to be given more direct access to information about the subject, this direct information remains twice removed from the viewer; the implication is that knowledge about AIDS must be kept secret, hidden–most important private. This, can easily be read as a further effort to maintain an association between AIDS and homosexuality, both of which cannot be directly represented as possibilities for a viewing audience that is being constructed as heterosexual, the "general public."

Beyond these general differences in the two sets of PSAs, specific PSAs in the CDC set offer important points of contrast that further illustrate the rhetorical maneuvers discussed in Chapter 3 that not only stigmatize gays, but position them and, more interestingly here, particular lifestyles as absolute other.

In three of the PSAs–"Diana, "Christina," and "Missy" (see Appendixes E, G, and I) – the talking heads appear with text in the lower right-hand corner of the screen that states the characters' names and the words "HIV Positive" beneath. This label for these characters obviously acts to define the characters in terms of sero-status; the effect is that identity comes to be based on, or at least associated with, a person's test results, results that, as Patton (1990b) points out, stigmatize gays and misplace responsibility. The HIV-positive label also conjures up images of quarantine and William Buckley's call to make people's, especially homosexuals' sero-status visible through body tattoos or brands.

Additionally, in the majority of PSAs analyzed, the central figure is a woman, who is represented as far removed from vampire-like images and postnuclear environments the culture associates with gays (with and without AIDS). The message, of course, is "anyone can get AIDS"–a key theme in the government's strategy to construct a "general public" for AIDS messages. However, much more is at stake here. First, there is an overabundance of emphasis on people who are stereotypically labeled as passive, sexually, as the responsible parties for the prevention and transmission of the disease. Given the cultural association of homosexuality with passive, recipient sex, there certainly seems to be a move that reinforces the link between AIDS and all that is not straight, active, masculine sex and sexuality. Second, in the messages' efforts to speak to the "general public" and reinforce the idea that heterosexual sex can also cause/result in AIDS, the messages reify a homo/hetero duality, suggest that heterosexuals are innocent victims–and the ones who merit concern and attention while homosexuals remain the guilty victims and cause of the disease–and, in effect, say that the time to become aware and responsible about the disease is when innocent heterosexuals become threatened. The homosexual is thus further depicted, by implication and omission, as abject and unrepresentable, just as he is in the Ad Council's messages.

In the "Sofa" PSA (see Appendix H), visibility is the issue of interest as a young, heterosexual couple are shown making out on a sofa. On a television set, positioned in front of the couple, an announcer claims, "Today, there's a good chance you know someone with HIV. People with HIV can look just as healthy as anyone else. You can't tell if someone is infected with the virus–just by looking." This message relies on the audience's fear of the other, the homosexual, the one who must be made visible–through testing/branding–in order for the audience to once again emerge capable of asserting a unified, coherent, fixed, and heterosexual self.

In addition to associations among homosexuality, the other,

disease, and quarantine seen in these "public health" messages, there is also a playing-out of the horror narrative discussed above and in Chapter 3. In two of the PSAs, "Christina" and "Missy" (see Appendixes G and I), the characters' narratives are organized around scenarios in which evil has entered their lives through no fault of their own: "I was really shocked when I found out I was infected. I didn't think anything like this could ever happen to me"; "People don't typically think of me as a person who would have HIV. But I do." These bits of narrative imply, like a 1950s science fiction film, that into the world of normalcy has come an alien invader that must be identified, separated from the general public, and stopped. So again homosexuals are narratively linked with impurity, germs, and images of invasion and infection.

Finally, one message, "HIV/Gary" (see Appendix F), in this set of PSAs is of particular interest here because it centers on a character that appears to be a representation of a gay man. Several points merit attention. First, how is the character represented as gay? What is it about his image that suggests marginality based on same sex desire? It is all a matter of stereotyping on the part of the message and the audience constructed by, interacting with, and making sense out of the message.

First, the scene opens with threatening music and a close-up of the talking head of a white man; the man says, "I was scared to take the HIV test. I knew once I did there was no turning back." The character has a soft-spoken voice, stereotypically associated with what is considered feminine, and his initial words suggest that he knew he was infected before he took the test. How? The culture's association of gay men with AIDS makes this characterization and construction of meaning not only possible, but imperative. Furthermore, there is no mention of sexual activity here; it cannot be named or represented, as it is in the other messages, both implicitly and explicitly. And the character and the audience are not positioned and coded to be shocked by the revelation that this man is HIV positive, because he was really labeled as such prior to the test.

In the next shot, following the character's premonition, the screen is filled with the following confirmational message: "Gary is infected with HIV, the virus that causes AIDS." The threatening music reaches a crescendo.

Then something quite interesting occurs. The music becomes more lighthearted; the camera shows medium and long shots of Gary on a bicycle riding through a countryside and then interacting with a woman. All seems well. The character's final words are: "Now I'm motivated to do things I've always wanted to do. Life seems so much more important now." What is being constructed here? The new gay man of the 1990s, it would seem. And this gay man, constructed for the "general public," possesses certain suspect qualities that make him visible: first, of course, he is HIV positive; second, because of his sero-status, his old ways and behaviors of homosexuality–those that cannot be represented in this message–have been discarded, replaced by a life that is sanitized, heterosexualized, but, most important, diametrically opposed to the irresponsible, unnatural, disco-driven, promiscuous gay life he must have known before–the lifestyle that is responsible for his infection. What emerges is a nonsexual gay man (a possibility?) who is able to more effectively manage his life. The problem, of course, as Schecter (1991) points out, is that without discourse and representations about sexuality, the gay voice is still positioned as other, but simultaneously prevented from speaking as other. Through this particular AIDS message, it appears that the government has managed, or attempted, to reverse the reverse discourse that contemporary gay communities have used to constitute political identities, as discussed in Chapter 2. Of course, in the context of the PSA messages, this move to use/usurp the communities' words for silencing purposes is represented as necessary for gay survival and merely educational in terms of a "public health" message from the government.

As stated before, with the silencing, and consequent defining, of the homosexual lifestyle, governmental discourse suggests that such lifestyle runs counter to healthy, safe, "normal" sexual activity. Thus, the prevention of AIDS is organized around and defined by acceptable sexual orientation rather than around the activity of safe sex. While the ads explicitly seem to offer general information on AIDS prevention and the need for awareness about safe sex, they implicitly advocate and define what is considered to be "natural" sexual preference and lifestyle. The government, therefore, defines what is considered to be an acceptable picture of healthy sexual activity. And, as seen with the earlier ads, AIDS is constituted as a disease that can be dealt with only for and by those who engage in sanctioned, nonanal, sexual practices that retain the active position of male power. Interestingly, the voice of the government is less present in the CDC's ads than it is in the Ad Council's ads. The CDC ads thus take on the voice of the people (the citizens) and the intrusion of the government's voice seems muffled.

It is important to note that, in the CDC ads, the prevention of AIDS is associated with talking about the disease. However, as noted earlier, when the characters begin to talk, the narrator takes over the discourse and provides a toll-free number that again empowers the government's discourse about AIDS. While talk seems to be the best and only way to prevent infection, the only talk sanctioned by the ad is that dialogue that occurs between literally or figuratively straight citizens and their government, which finally offers the perfect illustration of discourse as surveillance.

CONCLUSION

What becomes immediately apparent from these PSAs, as Watney (1987a) says in the previous chapter, is that the media construct something called a "general public," which privileges, and treats as natural and biological, the heterosexual family. All else, because it is denied a voice, is treated as disposable. One additional point worth noting here is that, while the federal government is charged with constructing messages that target and constitute the general public, gay community-based organizations are responsible for doing the same for gay communities. As Patton (1990b), quoted earlier, claims, this bifurcation of efforts assigns varying kinds and amounts of responsibilities to different audiences, and ultimately enacts further victimization on marginal communities.

The consequence of the above analysis is what Shapiro (1981 and 1984) calls the literary explication of the mythologizing process in discourse, which not only creates subjectivity, knowledge, and truth, but which creates them in a way that seems natural and incontrovertible.

> The literary reading reveals then a mythic story; it transforms an austerely written policy analysis into a legitimizing pamphlet, a celebration of part of the existing order (moreover, the part that is perhaps most difficult to celebrate from the point of view of values such as justice and fairness, etc.). This celebration is evident, not only when one takes the plot and the genre of the story as a whole. It is evident also when one does a closer, more detailed literary reading, paying attention to the lending discourses that govern the writing and produce kinds of subjects, objects and modes of conduct. (Shapiro, 1984, p. 246)

These literary details help to perpetuate a myth; as Frye says, "they help get the job done" (1973, p. 246). And, in fact, the PSAs from the advertising and governmental agencies do get the job done. Explicitly, the job is to educate; implicitly, and more important, the job is to define and advocate a lifestyle based on the binary division of sexual preference.

What the PSAs ultimately educate the general public about is how to identify the quintessential, and existential, menace of the twentieth century: anally driven, promiscuous gay men and the disease they spread. The "general public" is encouraged to make gays visible and subject to surveillance just as the PSA does— through depictions of disease and excrement.

At the beginning of the epidemic, gays realized quickly both the literal and representational danger AIDS posed. They also immediately assessed the marginalizing nature of the government's response, and its lack of direct action, that informs the construction of the "general public" in the PSAs discussed above.

In response, gays mounted a massive educational effort designed to fight against AIDS through empowerment messages designed by and spoken to gay communities. As discussed in Chapter 3, this educational effort was quite a radical response in the early years of the epidemic. However, after 1985, the government began to assert its influence over gay-focused and driven HIV prevention. The result has been a mainstreaming of what was once radical communication that sought to empower and give voice to gay communities.

The government's normalizing efforts in public health messages which construct the "general public" are expected, and often easy to identify. The government's influence on gay public health efforts, on the other hand, are much more complex: the radical voice certainly remains present, but its radical position is rendered problematic by the presence of institutional power. The next chapter explores the impact of this power on gay, community-based health education.

Chapter 5

The Cultural Construction of Marginal Identity in Community-Based AIDS/HIV Education

This chapter examines public health communication designed by and for gay communities. This analysis, which reports on a series of interviews with public health educators in Oklahoma charged with creating and implementing AIDS outreach to gays, focuses on public, private, and nonprofit attempts to reach the marginal group that is currently the most affected, and stigmatized, by the disease; importantly these messages work to reposition the marginal as central in public health communication. The analysis of these examples offers a cultural reading of community-based AIDS messages and an examination of governmental restrictions placed on public health campaigns that attempt to target, reach, define, and often restrict gay men and the information they receive.

It was essential that the state know what was happening with its citizens' sex, and the use they made of it, but also that each individual be capable of controlling the use he made of it. Between the state and the individual, sex became an issue,

An earlier version of this study appears as follows:

Myrick, R. (1995). "Communicating About Empowerment in an Environment of Silence: Public and Community-Based HIV and AIDS Education for Gay Men in Oklahoma," in L. Fuller and L. Shilling (eds.), *Communicating About Communicable Diseases*. Amherst: Human Resource Development Press. Reprinted by permission.

and a public issue no less; a whole web of discourses, special knowledges, analyses, and injunctions settled upon it. (Foucault, 1976/1990, p.26)

Safer sex should be a key agenda item for progressives, but it must be pursued in a context that gives control over how the safer sex message is articulated and how safer sex norms are enforced. It is hard to persuade those who do not yet engage in safer sex to do so if the state continues to have the power to arrest people for sodomy. (Patton, 1989, p. 244)

. . . brand-new state! Brand-new state
Gonna treat you great . . .

Plen'y of room to swing a rope!
Plen'y of heart and plen'y of hope. . .
                    (Hammerstein, 1943, pp. 131-132)

Talking about AIDS in Oklahoma is a very curious thing indeed. And while it remains crucially important to "de-gay" understandings and discussions of the HIV virus and AIDS as only and always linked to gay men and their sexual behaviors, AIDS education in Oklahoma remains centered on reaching gay men because of particular contextual discourses that often deny them a healthy space for being gay in the face of the AIDS pandemic. And these contextual discourses, which emanate from the state, the community, and the individual, must be acknowledged and negotiated in order to empower a gay voice. This voice is particularly important in a rather remote state like Oklahoma, which is often seen as an area of low risk because of the size of the gay communities and the number of reported AIDS cases; but the perception of Oklahoma as a low-risk area is the very reason why AIDS education of gay men is so important here. Health department reports to the state indicate that HIV cases continue to rise (Nyitray, 1995).

The purpose of this discussion is to look at the cultural consequences of traditional AIDS education for gay men; identify community-based programs nationwide that resist such traditional, stigmatizing, and usually ineffective approaches; examine specific programs for gays, both public and community-based, currently in place in Oklahoma; and, finally, comment on possible strategies of resistance that can be used in future efforts.

GAY RESPONSE TO CULTURAL STIGMATIZATION

One of the most important features of AIDS educational efforts for gays is the need to deconstruct existing public (straight) discourse, which treats gays as inherently destined to contract HIV. Thus, Crimp (1988b) argues that AIDS education must teach gays "how to be promiscuous in the age of AIDS," in order to avoid being subsumed by and into the moralistic discourse of straight society. And, in fact, GMHC's and SFAF's educational efforts are aimed at encouraging people to continue to have as much of the same kind of sex as they have always had, only to do so safely while maintaining eroticism (Palacios-Jiminez, 1989). While gayness is certainly not exclusively or essentially promiscuous, or anally driven, the possibilities that are part of gay liberation discourse must remain intact (Crimp, 1988b).

Treichler (1988) further argues that this opposition to dominant culture discourse is what gave shape to the gay liberation movement of the 1970s, which provided a foundation for gays to resist their positioning in the AIDS era. This approach emphasizes the presence of gay voices (as Yingling, 1991, describes) rather than the absence encouraged by straight culture.

In response to, and coincidental with, the culture's initial association of AIDS with homosexuality, gays began their own educational efforts in the early 1980's with groups such as GMHC and SFAF, both of which, as discussed earlier, seek to deal with AIDS education in sex-positive and identity-affirming discourse for gay communities (Valdiserri, 1989). These community-based educational efforts have been shown to positively influence behavioral changes in large urban communities (Stall, Coates, and Hoff, 1988). Such groups have also managed to maintain the combative communities that have remained coherent and essential to gay rights. (Patton, 1990b; 1988; 1985).

In general, and in the case of Oklahoma, these public health educational efforts employ a variety of approaches. Valdisseri (1989) cites five theoretical foundations of AIDS prevention efforts: cognitive development and decision making, learning theories, motivational emotional arousal, interpersonal relations including social influence, and communication/persuasion theories. Homans and Aggleton (1988) cite four models used in AIDS eduction that make use of one or more of these theories: behavior change-informational, self-empowerment, community orientation, and social transformation.

What have such community-based educational efforts focused on? Dejowski (1989) found that these efforts include supportive social norms, awareness of the individual within a larger environment, and explicit safer sex messages that remain sensitive to the needs of gay men, messages that cannot be federally funded because of restrictions resulting from the 1988 Helms amendment. Schernoff and Palacios-Jimenez (1988) added to this list the importance of treating AIDS, in educational efforts targeted for gay men, as a behavioral, not a group-based, disease to alleviate internalized stigma. Stall, Coates, and Hoff (1988) cite other conditions conducive to behavioral change, such as the use of drugs/alcohol during sexual contact, general health beliefs, and personal efficacy. Finally, Kelley et al. (1992) found that endorsement and promotion of safe sex by popular, influential people in gay communities help produce behavioral changes.

In short, simple informational campaigns aimed at gay people are not enough. Only a combination of approaches designed and implemented by gay communities can accomodate the needs of effective education. The above approaches constitute the strategies that were initially and are currently being used by gays in an effort to take control of and create their own educational response to HIV and AIDS. However, as radical and empowering as these strategies were and continue to be, significantly, they have also been professionalized, and coopted by the government since its entrance into the field of HIV public health education after 1985. What follows is an illustration of how these conflicting forces coexist in current HIV prevention efforts.

THE CULTURAL CONTEXT OF OKLAHOMA

It is important to be aware of the cultural contexts associated with Oklahoma. First, the state is situated in the Bible Belt, and a recent study of the attitudes of highly religous people in Oklahoma has shown that they tend to be extremely prejudiced against and unsupportive of civil rights for gay people (Garner, Hardesty, and Wenk, 1992). This became salient for gay educational efforts when Tim Pope, a state representative, spread fear throughout public-based organizations when he claimed that "straight" taxpayers' dollars were being spent on explicit, pornographic materials that promote deviant (read "homosexual") practices, because the state health department had ordered *one* copy of a sexually explicit educational comic for study.

Second, because of the often repressive environment for gays in Oklahoma, many remain closeted and silent to avoid the loss of jobs and homes and maintain personal rights and safety. This imposed silence, when combined with an overwhelmingly religious environment, prevents many gays from experiencing a sense of community with other gays, thus limiting self-esteem and educational exposure.

Third, the state health department has undergone a series of changes in administrative positions (Hinton, 1992) due to a CDC investigation of the ability of the state's AIDS educational efforts to reach gay populations. This inability to effectively and com-

prehensively reach gay communities, in turn, is often the consequence of the competition for funds by various community-
based organizations, the state department's response to political
personalities, and fear of funding reductions (discussed in more
detail below).

Fourth, while it would be highly inaccurate to report that there
is no sense of community for gays in Oklahoma (at least in large
cities), or that educational efforts are not reaching or are not
targeted toward gays, the sense of community and the communities that are being reached are largely centered around strips of
bars, which community organizers who were interviewed for this
discussion claim represent a minority of gays in Oklahoma. And,
most important, while cumulative state reports as of June, 1995,
cite 2,307 cases of AIDS in Oklahoma and 1,538 HIV-positive
persons (Nyitray, 1995), community educators estimate the number of HIV-positive persons to be 10,000, because people who
are afraid of testing are not counted and because the state reports
only the results of confidential testing; anonymous testing is not
reported (personal interviews, November-December 1992 and
January 1993, cited below individually).

STATE- AND COMMUNITY-BASED EDUCATIONAL
PROGRAMS FOR GAYS

These are the restrictive conditions that frame the "swinging of
gay men's ropes" in Oklahoma. What follows is a discussion of
how public and community educational organizers responded to
these restrictions in a series of personal, and at times contradictory interviews. Public responses include those of the Oklahoma
State Department of Health (HIV Division) and the University of
Oklahoma College of Medicine. Community-based responses include those of the Tulsa Oklahomans for Human Rights, Oklahoma's ACT UP organization, and the Triangle Association. Direc-
tors at the OASIS Resource Center and Red Rock Mental Health

Center were also interviewed but are not included in this discussion because their organizations' activities are similar to those of the other community-based organizations mentioned above. These interviewees represent all of the state's educational programs that are directed primarily toward gays and lesbians. These interviews indicate that the response of both public and community-based organizations has been mixed, for various reasons.

STATE EDUCATIONAL PROGRAMS

State Health Department

In Oklahoma, federal funds for education are funneled through the state health department, which decides who gets funding and what that funding can be used for, given both federal and state restrictions. In and attempt by the state to posit a gay audience, Alan Nyitray (1992) was hired in 1989 as the coordinator of gay/lesbian outreach for the HIV-STD Service Division of the state health department. Nyitray's responsibilities include gay/ lesbian outreach, primarily in the Oklahoma City area; Tulsa outreach programs were, at the time of these interviews, contracted out to the University of Oklahoma College of Medicine and to Tulsa Oklahomans for Human Rights, a private, nonprofit organization. According to Nyitray, two strategies guide the health department's efforts, and ultimately represent and discursively enact gay identity for the state: (a) free and easy access to condoms through distribution to the most frequented and concentrated outlets in high-profile gay community areas and (b) education for gays on safe sex.

In light of Foucault (1976/1990; 1984/1990; 1984/1988), and Schecter's (1991) appropriation, the state targets and constitutes a very particular gay person as the recipient of gay outreach: gays attending bars. Certainly alcohol-oriented environments where much cruising occurs are in need of free and easy access to condoms; however, what is particularly compelling here is that by limiting its efforts primarily to gays who are cruising in bars, the state's educational program discursively constitutes gays as promiscuous. Those who are most likely to receive governmental support in the form of education are gays who identify themselves as the state does. The state's target audience exemplifies Schecter's (1991) discussion of the double-bind situation in which gay men find themselves in the context of AIDS. Gays are constituted existentially as engaging in unsafe behavior, defined by the state as promiscuous anal sex, but can neither engage in nor talk about that behavior. Given Schecter's (1991) account of the two men who fail to pick each other up in the bar, because sex is nothing without talk, gay identity is constituted by the government in a way that actually establishes an isomorphic relationship between anonymous, anally driven sexual activity and what culture constitutes as male homosexuality. Gay identity, at the hands of the state, is thus effectively linked with death and absence, as Schecter (1991) argues.

The state's strategies are implemented in a number of ways. First, Nyitray distributes condoms to gay clubs in the city. (Interestingly, even among people at gay community bars, reactions to the public display of HIV prevention efforts such as condoms ranges from enthusiastic to resistant, reactions that the state depends on for its marginal representations of gays.) Nyitray insists that public display of condoms is crucial for sending a sex-positive message to the gay communities about condom use and, therefore, resists placing condoms in bar restrooms, which would connote secrecy and privatization. It is important, Nyitray claims, that safe sex be made public, accessible, and everyday. Of course, while this is sex-positive, it also works to further codify and control sex by making it visible, definable, and subject to discourse, an essential element of contemporary sexuality according to Foucault's analysis of repression.

Nyitray also conducts demonstrations in bars about the correct and erotic ways condoms can be used, and indeed one of his most important messages is that safe sex "feels good." In his outreach to gay communities, Nyitray stresses healthy sexuality, rather than the dangers of the disease, never telling people that certain sex acts are bad, even unprotected anal sex. But he makes it clear that with certain unprotected sexual activities people are entering a risky environment. Nyitray claims that this sex-positive approach is crucial, both for bringing effective HIV and AIDS education to gays and for the maintenance of gay sexualities, as the bedroom has typically been the refuge of gay men, where they experience control over their lives.

These strategies provide compelling evidence that Nyitray, on one level, is clearly sensitive to political, social, and existential issues faced by many gay men; his educational approach is sex-positive and erotic, and he uses this approach to empower gay voices, a strategy that mirrors that early efforts used by GMHC. But while the health department deploys "health, sex-positive" HIV prevention education, it simultaneously prohibits education that is explicitly sexual or supportive of gay experiences, an integral part of effective education.

The health department obtains most of its educational materials from the GMHC and the SFAF, the largest distributors of these materials for gays. But any pamphlets paid for with public monies must be approved by a state review board; and, while the board-approved list of materials is fairly inclusive, Nyitray said the HIV-STO Service Division cannot fund the production of sexually explicit materials because of the 1988 Helms amendment. The restrictions on explicit materials effectively negate the possible effectiveness, as well as the original focus on the posited gay audience, of erotic safer sex messages designed by the GMHC's educational program.

Furthermore, prohibitive internal and external scrutiny of the health department has limited in-house publishing to one pamphlet—*Considering an Oklahoma Cruise?* (Oklahoma State

Department of Health, 1992a). Produced and distributed by the health department, it discusses safe sex in a visually stimulating but alternately clinical and metaphoric way, guiding the reader through a fictional cruise-ship experience–intended to be a metaphor for cruising for sex. Although "anal sex," "penises," and "cum" are mentioned in the pamphlet, along with directions for effective condom use, the language is often veiled and includes the sex-negative rhetoric that "the more cruises you take with different partners, the more likely it is you'll sink." The sterile and metaphoric discursive strategies used to depict gay sexual experiences in the pamphlet strip away gay desire and represent gay identity antierotically. Gaining state authority to produce the "cruising" pamphlet took two years, and even then it had to be printed through a community organization so that the state department's name would not appear on the pamphlet. In an attempt to negotiate such restrictions, the state health department often brokers out services, such as printing jobs, on a contractual basis to community organizations. This allows for printing and distribution of materials that the state department might deem appropriate but would not want its name explicitly associated with. However, given the restrictive environment in which it operates, exemplified by the one sterilized message that the state managed to produce, negotiation attempts merely add to the bureaucracy, which hinders effective outreach to gays, reinforces further marginalization, and culturally defines gays only in terms of straight discourse.

For the future, Nyitray is concerned with an increased focus on substance abuse, gay/lesbian youth, and gay/lesbian people of color. But since Tim Pope's alarmism, the state health department has pushed Nyitray to disassociate the department from the gay/lesbian community, at least explicitly. The main reason for the push for disassociation is the department's fear of funding cuts because of local fears and attitudes toward gays and gay lifestyles. Outcries such as Tim Pope's (and Foucault would say these outcries and consequential threats essentially constitute the state as a palpable entity) may ultimately threaten funds from the federal government, particularly if the state health department is thought to be in violation of the Helms amendment. Thus, the argument can be made by the state that technical, medical, and ultimately straight, nonsexual outreach (which has been found to be ineffective) is the most that can be done.

The University of Oklahoma —College of Medicine

The University of Oklahoma College of Medicine's Tulsa Health Education and Risk Reduction Outreach (THERRO) was the other of the state's two public organizations providing gay/ lesbian HIV prevention programs. But Sandy Hill (1992), the director of the organization, received notice on the day of this interview that all state and federal funds would be eliminated for THERRO; the organization closed one month later. An analysis of the organization's activities and its loss of funding remains particularly interesting, however, in light of Hill's approach to AIDS education.

The organization was a rebellious force within the state's effort. Hill asserted that her organization offered the most effective gay and lesbian outreach in the state and was one of the most progressive HIV educational programs in middle America. Hill suggested that one of the reasons her organization was being shut down was because it did not fit with the conservative context of the university, the state health department, and/or the federal government.

Part of what made THERRO'S approach radical was Hill's insistence on treating HIV prevention holistically; in other words, she educated people about their overall lifestyles in order to strengthen immune system defenses. Hill managed this by connecting people with a variety of service organizations throughout the city. One such organization was the HIV Resource Consortium, a one-stop center for education, networking, testing, medical and social services, and general support for gays in a nonthreatening atmosphere. Care teams were also in place to provide services to PLWAs.

And Hill's own organization, enabled largely by the efforts of 35 volunteers, offered HIV education/prevention/testing/counseling to multiple subpopulations in gay and lesbian communities throughout Tulsa, communities the state health department avoids. Educational and testing services were taken to low-income housing complexes, a Tulsa park frequented by gay men, university organizations, and gay clubs, where Hill had been known to show up in a condom hat to attract clients' attention, certainly a very queer approach to public health education. For club appearances on special occasions, Hill coordinated a group of people who, calling themselves "condom crusaders," dressed in black-and-white capes and rushed into bars to pass out safe sex kits and to educate people about her organization. Hill also conducted educational sessions in private homes for professional organizations in Tulsa, many of whose members remained closeted, and safe sex parties in private citizens' homes. What can be seen here that is different from the state health department's approach is the organization's attempt to broaden the definition of gay sexualities by focusing on other areas in addition to bars for outreach.

One obvious concern about Hill's overall educational push was its inclusion of testing as a key part of HIV prevention; for gays, the stigmatizing association between education and testing certainly renders THERRO's methods problematic, a compelling illustration of the influence of the state's control and power. While Hill's broader and more contextual approach discursively constituted gay identity and AIDS education in a more inclusive, and less technical, way than did the state health department, a key component of this inclusivity was the technical, stigmatizing act of testing.

THERRO's educational materials also treated gay sex fairly

generically, providing much of the same literature found in most of the gay and lesbian HIV outreach organizations in Oklahoma City, including several pamphlets with erotic (through nonexplicit) covers of gay men embracing, Red Cross literature, several pamphlets and booklets on general health habits. Hill said the generic nature of the printed literature was due largely to the state's lack of awareness regarding gay cultural needs. The health department's "cruising" pamphlet was probably the most explicit piece of material available. In terms of printed textual material, then, gay sexualities are again being constituted technically and antierotically; given the needs of gays for effective safe sex education, the literature fails to reach the marginal audience.

Overall, THERRO's outreach was certainly more comprehensive and diverse in its treatment and construction of gay and lesbian audiences than the state health department's efforts, and, at least according to Hill, this posed a real threat to state government that insisted on treating gay communities in fixed, monolithic, and stigmatizing ways. Still, even an approach like Hill's that may have appeared radical to the state was unable to completely separate itself from the influence of government.

COMMUNITY-BASED EDUCATION
FOR GAYS AND LESBIANS

The presence and control of public funding and the voice of the state are also felt by the gay/lesbian community organizations across the state—four in Oklahoma City and one in Tulsa—although the extent of this funding and resulting restrictions vary.

Tulsa Oklahomans for Human Rights

Tulsa Oklahomans for Human Rights (TOHR), for instance, has existed as a private, nonprofit organization for some time, but has only since 1992 received state money for assistance for gay/lesbian outreach. And, while its state-funded educational materials must appear on the state's approved list, director Ric Kirby (1992) reports that TOHR brings in enough money through donations, newsletter subscriptions, and fund-raising to support itself with minimal help from the state, thereby allowing greater freedom from governmental restrictions. The most obvious example of this freedom is TOHR's use of a highly direct and explicit pamphlet, *Mansex: Do It Right* (NO-AIDS Task Force, 1992). It uses terms such as "fucking," "sucking," and "rimming," with no mention of a metaphoric "cruise." This pamphlet is clear, memorable, and effective for its audience, and it is certainly representative of what safer sex messages could say when state money and the politics that guide the use of such funds are not involved. This pamphlet is an example of the kind of erotically charged AIDS message produced by GMHC, and unlike the state's pamphlet its message deconstructs the scientific attempt to medicalize gays and AIDS; instead, safe sex becomes intrinsically connected with what is identified as homoerotic desire.

TOHR also provides education and a host of other in-house services for people with HIV and AIDS: social workers, religious services, help for the homeless, social security services, banking opportunities, and a food bank. In addition, members offer social opportunities for gays and lesbians in nonbar environments. Like THERRO, TOHR's comprehensive approach to HIV prevention constitutes gay and lesbian identity much more diversely than the state health department; of course, like THERRO, TOHR also offers and promotes onsight testing as a key part of its overall effort, so diversity again becomes linked to the marginalizing act of testing, of making gays visible for the government and ultimately straight culture.

ACT UP Oklahoma

Compared to Tulsa, Oklahoma City has more unified, open, and active gay/lesbian communities, as evidenced by the presence of its small but vocal ACT UP organization, the only one in the state. According to Smithson and Steeves (1992), two of four core members of ACT UP, the organization receives no public funding from the state, allowing it to retain the explicitness of its messages.

Recently and historically, ACT UP's main educational efforts have focused on safer sex presentations for college classes at the University of Oklahoma, various civic organizations, and gay/ lesbian college group meetings. At the time of this interview, the group had reached approximately 5,000 college students in a two-year period. Although Smithson and Steeves adjust their messages, language, and visuals to reach (and, Foucault would argue, to constitute,) different audiences, their discussions are always frank and emphatic. The pair reveal that one of the most effective and radical aspects of their presentations is that Smithson, openly discusses what his life is like as an HIV-positive individual. Smithson said this personalizes the issue for audiences by presenting them with someone who looks "normal" but who has in fact constantly battled opportunistic infections and takes approximately 30 pills daily. Through the efforts of ACT UP, AIDS becomes embodied for both straight and gay audiences–an educative and definitional position other state-sponsored organizations avoid.

ACT UP has also produced pamphlets for different groups within both gay/lesbian and straight communities. Funds for these pamphlets, and indeed all of ACT UP's monies, come from donations and merchandise sales. Beyond this, the group relies on the help of friends for use of facilities and resources to subsidize materials needed for safe sex packets and printing costs. The state department has supplied the group with free condoms for distribution, but at the time of this interview, ACT UP was told that this would end in the next year. What can be seen in ACT UP's approach is the kind of gay and lesbian community effort initially offered by GMHC.

Smithson and Steeves (1992) identify five factors affecting behavioral and attitudinal change that guide their educational approaches: educational background, available resources, having previously had a sexually transmitted disease, self-esteem, and having known someone who died of AIDS. Because fewer people have died of AIDS in Oklahoma than in states initially hit hard by HIV/AIDS cases, the pair feel change has been slow to come about. Still, they aim at reducing unsafe behavior, even if they can't completely eliminate it. So, with only four core members (as community organizers have said, the Oklahoma gay communities are just not very politically active) and no public funds, ACT UP continues to offer one of the most explicit, positive, and substantive educational efforts in the state. Their approach is particularly radical because of Smithson's ability to deconstruct the categories of gay and straight by embodying the syndrome as human. Of course, the scope of ACT UP's outreach is limited by minimal resources.

Triangle Association

Finally, the Triangle Association is a community-based, non-profit organization that has been in Oklahoma City since 1984. Administered by volunteer Dr. Larry Prater, the Triangle Association offers one of the first HIV prevention programs in the state, a food bank that services the Oklahoma City area, a free clinic for HIV-positive people and PLWAs, and one of the most heavily used HIV prevention and testing facilities in the state designed specifically for gay men, Testing the Limits. The Triangle Association is also funded primarily with state controlled money. As such, Prater's organization provides the most striking example of gay empowering HIV prevention in Oklahoma, despite and through the support of the state.

While several of the organizations discussed above provide comprehensive approaches to HIV education and, thereby, constitute gay identity in complex and diverse ways, Prater's is the most radical in its insistence on the celebration of multiple gay sexualities. For example, the walls of the Triangle Association are covered with sexually explicit posters of gay men and lesbians engaged in safe and erotic sex; the men and women pictured are racially and ethnically diverse, and the scenes depicted include a variety of sexual interests and positionings including leather, cowboy, S/M and a multiplicity of acts such as oral, anal, and nongenital sex. The association also provides gay and lesbian cultural and political literature and videotapes of safe sex messages and gay pornography for visitors to view while they wait for clinic services.

At one point, Prater was actually arrested on an obscenity charge for the sexual explicitness of his educational materials, a charge of which he was eventually acquitted. The fact that the local district attorney was willing to press charges, an action that received heavy publicity throughout the city and was even reported nationally and internationally, illustrates Prater's general demeanor as an activist and his position as an AIDS educator. He combats institutional power that opposes his radical, sex-positive political and educational position; and this combative position empowers gays to speak out not only for their survival, but for their happiness and satisfaction.

The Triangle Association facility has, consequently, become a kind of community center, at least for white gay males. Recently, Prater even used the Triangle Association to host showings of gay and lesbian art that attracted people from a variety of area gay and lesbian communities.

Prater also employs unconventional outreach located in areas of Oklahoma City where anonymous public sex takes place, often among men who don't necessarily identify themselves as gay. He uses a team of educators called "Bushwhackers" to deliver condoms, lubrication, and safe sex literature directly to men who are about to engage in sex in public places.

In general, the Triangle Association offers the most comprehensive, progressive, and explicitly politicized gay outreach program in the state. However, Prater's approach to education is strongly tied to HIV testing. When discussing Triangle and its accomplishments, Prater defines the organization by pointing to the fact that it tested 82 percent of all those tested for HIV in Oklahoma from 1988 to 1990. Of course one of the reasons Prater makes this association is because, until quite recently, the CDC required that federally funded education be connected with testing. Looking back to the earlier discussion of Foucault's (1976/1990) analysis of the origins of the "care of the self," it is easy to see that the emphasis on testing discrusively encourages gays to sterilize and technologize sexual behavior and categorize sexual diversity, thus as Schecter (1991) claims, speaking themselves into silence and ultimately absence. But Prater's educational approach is also heavily reliant on eroticized and explicit safer sex behavior, which mirrors the radical approach of GMHC.

Understandably, Dr. Prater and the state health department have a somewhat uneasy relationship, which further illustrates Triangle's paradoxical nature. Over the years, Dr. Prater has fought the health department through the Centers for Disease Control, personally and in the courts, because he claims the department is failing in its educational mission to gays. Prater claims that it is because of these battles that the Triangle Association, which relies heavily on funding from the state for its survival, receives much less money and fewer opportunities than other community organizations that reach a fraction of the people Triangle reaches. For instance, Prater said that in 1991, when the Triangle Association administered 41 percent of the HIV tests in Oklahoma—a period during which community-based educational funds were tied to HIV testing—it received only 6 percent of the state's allocations for community organizations. In 1992, when the Triangle Association continued to provide approximately half of the HIV tests in the state, it received only 12 percent of state funds, much less than other organizations performing fewer tests.

As radical as Prater's erotic safe sex messages are, and this is limited given state funding restrictions, when he justifies his organization and his efforts, he constitutes gay identities in technical, instrumental, and quantifiable terms set out by the state: the agency's merits are often determined by the number of tests that have been administered, and people's identities are often associated with sero-status. On the other hand, it can be argued that Prater uses state definitions to deconstruct the state's sterile representations of gays and obtain funding for erotic messages that the state would not endorse.

According to ACT UP's Smithson (1992), who also serves as the director of the Triangle Association Testing the Limits tests and counsels approximately 300 people per month, mainly from the gay community. Approximately 200 to 250 additional individuals come in just for educational and safer sex materials. The center operates with 12 to 15 steady volunteers and one full-time paid position. As in other organizations, pamphlets purchased with health department money must meet state and federal requirements; however, if Smithson sees something he considers to be effective that is not on the list, he will produce his own version, a practice that seems to attest to the deconstructive nature of this organization on one level. The newest pamphlets ordered emphasize self-esteem issues for gay men to encourage low-risk behavior. In the future, Smithson expects the state to provide the Triangle Association with additional funds for outreach to parks, bars, and for condom supplies for the state. However, Prater said that the Triangle Association has been notified that these funds may go to the OASIS Center, an informational and referral facility in Oklahoma City, despite the fact that the Triangle Association is currently doing more work in HIV and

AIDS education and prevention than any other organization in the state.

Prater claims that health department officials resent his criticism, and seem to take their resentment out on him by directing funds to programs that do not reach as many people as does the Triangle Association. He cites the following as an example: the CDC gave the state $300,000 for HIV and AIDS education and prevention programs in 1992, of which the state earmarked $90,000 for gay outreach programs. The state gave half of these funds to Red Rock Mental Health Center, another gay/lesbian outreach organization, focusing on the coordination of gay/lesbian youth support groups, which Prater claims has done little more with the money than local advertising for its youth services. For Prater, this allocation of funds is symptomatic of the state's illogical and ineffective allocation of funds and of its utter disregard for gay men. In 1993, Prater complained to CDC officials in Atlanta, and, following an investigation, the state health department reorganized its HIV division, brought in new administration, and cut out one level of bureaucracy.

In sum, the most radical organization in terms of fighting and manipulating state control, and in terms of producing and constituting gay sex as erotic–thus maintaining the political power of the gay voice as other–is the same organization that discursively links gay identity in the wake of AIDS with the instrumental effect of testing. Herein lies the ultimate paradox for gay, community-based, governmental-funded HIV prevention: even though Prater has adopted the government's techniques for defining gay identity, his approach remains fundamentally celebratory and empowering of diverse relationships within gay communities, and, therefore, his organization fails to receive the funds for which it qualifies. This illustrates the situation in which gay community educators find themselves: it is not enough to adopt the state's technical, stigmatizing, test-based guidelines to define and determine the scope, merit, and substance of HIV prevention for gays; educators must also avoid education, like Prater's, that attempts to empower gay communities in a fundamental way.

Conclusion

Of those testing HIV positive in Oklahoma from 1991 to 1992 gay men account for at least 76 percent (Oklahoma State Department of Health, 1992b). As of 1995, of those persons with AIDS in Oklahoma, 78 percent are men who report having sex with other men (Nyitray, 1995). Reasons include a conservative culture and environment, political battles among community organizations and with the state for funds, ineffective allocation of funds by the state, the gay population's battle with self-esteem, and the perception that Oklahoma is a low-risk area (or the wish that it be one).

While the federal and state departments of health decide on issues of funding and message/educational content, the gay communities in Oklahoma have fought to create a network of support and resistance to their own genocide and to foster a healthier context in which to live. The problem that remains is that the more the culture, including both straight and gay identified constituencies, talks about gays in state-supported programs, the further from liberation and radicalness gays find themselves. So, as Schecter (1991) argues, gays are encouraged to talk in Oklahoma, but that talk, at least when it is controlled by the state, must not endorse or speak about sexual diversity.

COMPARISON OF PSA MESSAGES AND COMMUNITY-BASED APPROACHES TO AIDS EDUCATION

The above analyses of two approaches to AIDS education contain some important points of comparison and contrast.

First, the community-based approaches are representative of the kinds of messages that gays are constructing for their own survival. They stand in stark contrast to the messages constructed for the general public in the PSA messages. Most obviously, gay men actually exist as human producers, audience members, and characters in the community-based messages; in the PSAs, gays remain representational only as infectious "other" encroaching on innocent heterosexuals. Second, in the community messages, gay identity is constructed erotically, and through diverse relational and sexual positioning; in the PSA messages, gay identity is constructed as essentially destructive and diseased. And, finally, the community messages are organized around and employ strategies that empower gays in the face of AIDS; the PSAs further enact on gays the crisis of representation that has been in place in dominant culture for the last 150 years. So in a sense community-based education is reconstructing gay identity in life-affirming ways.

Strikingly, however, the community-based messages are as problematic as they are pro-gay. In subtle ways, the influence of mainstream forces inevitably comes to encroach upon marginal communication, and associations between gay desire and disease recur. For example, community-based messages that represent gay identity in a general sense as erotic and central often concurrently represent safe sex, particular sexual activities, and certain lifestyles in ways that follow the lead of moralistic, prohibitive, and sex-negative communication propagated by the federal government and the culture at large. Additionally, there is a tendency in some community-based approaches to associate safe sex with HIV testing, which, for gay men, evokes images of labeling and quarantine, a move that works to remedicalize gay desire.

What remains most compelling about these findings is that such associations are more insidious than they are in the blatantly mainstream PSA messages. Why? Community-based education, even when it associates gay identity with death and disease, appears to be, and often is, communication that empowers marginal voices. The conditions for marginal communication ultimately emerge as paradoxical, empowering on the surface, but implicitly oppressive.

The community-based messages in Oklahoma also rely heavily on federal funding, which creates more obvious, though no less harmful, restrictions on community-based education that result in communication that is often generic, inexplicit, and, given the treatment of gays in this culture, harmful–just as harmful as the more explicitly negative messages in the PSAs. Furthermore, procedures for producing and distributing federally funded, community-based messages are frequently hampered by governmental bureaucracy and state-level legislative bodies. Ultimately, because of governmental intervention, the continuation of community-based education is often tied up with increasingly insidious associations between sexual diversity and disease. The consequence here is that gays, under the guise of economic survival of community-based education, are being encouraged to participate in their own sterilization. At least when gays are represented as infectious in the PSAs, it is fairly clear where they stand. With similar systems of meaning at work, however, in gay-driven, community-based approaches, the possibility for identification and resistance to continuing crises in representation is greatly diminished.

Chapter 6

Conclusion

What has been attempted in these pages is an examination and explication of a theory of power. The book examines cultural theorists who have made use of this theory to understand representations of marginal identity and disease, and government-controlled messages that enact relationships and representations that police, survey, and construct bodies, desires, and identities. It is no great surprise that PSAs produced by the federal government create an innocent "general public" that has a right to know about the disease of the other, stigmatizing the homosexual and representing him as an essential threat to mainstream systems of meaning. It is somewhat surprising, but more disturbing, that gay communities' educative, behavioral, and existential responses, responses that seemed radical to their remedicalization in the early 1980s, have by the 1990s often been professionalized, institutionalized, and co-opted by governmentally influenced public health campaigns.

It is heartening, though, that gay and lesbian politics have taken on celebratory, postmodern, "queer" agenda and civil rights efforts that are working to make the movements more inclusive of diverse marginal groups and that are producing art, literature, media, languages, bodies, identities–in short, cultures– that speak to and create new sexualities and erotic relationships such as the ones Foucault imagined.

It is also heartening that more than a decade into a disease that has been constructed to annihilate, physically and representationally, gay men, Foucault's analysis of sexuality continues to provide a political strategy for resistance against that annihilation. Hughes (1993) offers a compelling example of this strategic resistance in his reading of AIDS and 1990s disco, a reading that synthesizes the central issues of this book: power, discourse, marginal identity, and sexuality. His analysis is deployed, not as a way of escaping AIDS–which may finally be inescapable–but as a way to exist, erotically and powerfully, in spite of it.

> So if the AIDS epidemic almost killed disco in the late '80's, the same crisis has inspired its determined resurgence in the early '90's–after years of staying home, men want to go out and dance again. The revival is not simply nostalgia but an application of the discourse of disco to a new end. Recent songs celebrate the pleasurable discipline of self-exhaustion with all the brashness of early disco, unintimidated by the inevitable resonances set off by the epidemic . . . using it up and wearing it out on the dance floor may seem uncannily like submitting to the debilitation wrought by the virus; shaking our bodies down at a disco is pleasurable, while being shaken down by the health-care system is not. But surrender to the beat can briefly vaccinate us against fear. Once again gay men can defiantly appropriate and inoculate their society's most ruthless disciplines as their own means of survival . . . the music that once taught some men to be gay can now teach them what all gay men must learn: how to live with AIDS. Like safe sex or ACT UP or the concept of sexual identity itself, this indispensable discipline celebrates submission without acquiescence. Disco now looks forward to a moment when gay men can once again, vocally and unequivocally, say of their sexuality what Diana Ross once sang about her "love hangover": "If there's a cure for this, I don't want it." (Hughes, 1993, p. 21)

APPENDIXES

Appendix A

Transcript for Ad Council
PSA # 1/"Ocean"/:30/1991

(Scene opens with a slow pan and close-up zoom-in shot of a heterosexual teenaged couple making out on a beach as threatening music plays.)

Voice-over Narrator: Tonight, Dolores had a few drinks, did some crack, and ended up another tragic story, only she doesn't know it yet. Drugs can make you forget. And if you forget how risky sex can be, you can catch the AIDS virus and not know it for months or even years. AIDS – another way drugs can kill.

(Text fills the screen: "AIDS – ANOTHER WAY DRUGS CAN KILL"; underneath this text is the Ad Council, National Institute of Drug Abuse and U. S. Department of Health and Human Services' identification. A twenty-second version of this spot features the same message but omits the underlined phrase above.)

Note: In all of the appendixes, boldfaced print indicates explanatory comments made in addition to actual transcripts.

Appendix B

Transcript for Ad Council
PSA # 2/"Car"/:30/1991

(Scene opens with a zoom-in shot of a car parked, possibly crashed, at the side of a deserted road, with the taillights flashing on and off; threatening music plays.)

Voice-over Narrator: Tony had some drinks, a few joints, and got into a fatal accident tonight, only he doesn't know it yet. Drugs can make you forget. And if you forget how risky sex can be, you can catch the AIDS virus <u>and not know it for months or even years</u>. AIDS – another way drugs can kill.

(Text fills the screen: "AIDS – ANOTHER WAY DRUGS CAN KILL"; underneath this text is the Ad Council, National Institute of Drug Abuse, and U. S. Department of Health and Human Services' identification. A twenty-second version of this spot features the same message but omits the underlined phrase above.)

Appendix C

Transcript for Ad Council
PSA #3/"Roof"/:30/1991

(Scene opens with camera moving up the stairs of a deserted building to a roof; threatening music plays.)

Voice-over Narrator: This is where they partied, where Denise met Michael. They danced, they joked, they did a little crack and went up here, where she took the wrong step that ended everything, only she doesn't know it yet. Drugs make you forget. <u>And if you forget how risky sex can be, you can catch the AIDS virus and not know it for years</u>. AIDS – another way drugs can kill.

(Text fills the screen: "AIDS – ANOTHER WAY DRUGS CAN KILL"; underneath this text is the Ad Council, National Institute of Drug Abuse, and U. S. Department of Health and Human Services' identification. A twenty-second version of this spot features the same message but substitutes the following phrase for the one underlined above: "things, like how to prevent AIDS.")

Appendix D

Transcript of CDC PSA #1/"STD Woman"/:30/1991

(Scene opens with a close-up of a woman's talking head.)

Character: If you've had a sexually transmitted disease like gonorrhea, herpes, or syphilis – listen. What you were doing that exposed you to that disease could also expose you to the AIDS virus.

(Text fills the screen: "HIV is the virus that causes AIDS.")

Character: You are living proof that an STD can happen. Please don't prove it again.

Voice-over Narrator: Find out about HIV, the virus that causes AIDS.

("AMERICA RESPONDS TO AIDS" logo fills the screen, followed by a toll-free phone number and the CDC identification.)

Appendix E

Transcript of CDC
PSA #2/"Diana"/:10/1991

(Scene opens with a medium shot of a woman talking. The following text appears in the lower right-hand corner of the screen: "Diana, HIV Positive.")

Character: I'm a good example of how you can get AIDS from heterosexual sex.

Voice-over Narrator: Find out more about HIV, the virus that causes AIDS.

("AMERICA RESPONDS TO AIDS" logo fills the screen, followed by a toll-free phone number and the CDC identification.)

Appendix F

Transcript of CDC
PSA #3/"HIV-Gary"/:30/1991

(Scene opens with a close-up of a white man talking. Threatening music plays in the background.)

Character: I was scared to take the HIV test. I knew once I did there was no turning back.

(Text fills the screen: "Gary is infected with HIV, the virus that causes AIDS." Camera then pulls back and shows medium and long shots of character riding a bike and interacting with a woman. Music becomes more lighthearted.)

Character: Now that I know, though, I can get on with my life, make some goals. I'm working to stay healthy, thinking about going back to school.

(Text fills the screen: "Today, early treatment of HIV can mean a longer life." Camera returns to a medium shot of the man talking.)

Character: Now I'm motivated to do things I've always wanted to do. Life seems so much more important now.

Voice-over Narrator: For information on the prevention and treatment of HIV, call this toll-free number.

("AMERICA RESPONDS TO AIDS" logo fills the screen, followed by a toll-free phone number and the CDC identification.)

Appendix G

Transcript of CDC
PSA # 4/"Christina"/:20/1991

(Scene opens with a montage of black-and-white shots of men and women from various ethnic backgrounds saying, "It's not going to happen to me." Then camera cuts to a medium shot of a woman talking. The following text appears in the lower right-hand corner of the screen: "Christina: HIV Positive.")

Character: I was really shocked when I found out I was infected. I didn't think anything like this could ever happen to me.

(Text fills the screen: "If you're tired of thinking about HIV, listen to someone who's really sick of it." Then "AMERICA RESPONDS TO AIDS" logo fills the screen, followed by a toll-free phone number and the CDC identification.)

Appendix H

Transcript of CDC
PSA #5/"Sofa"/:30/1991

(Scene opens with a medium close-up of a young, heterosexual couple making out on a sofa. In the background, on a television set, a announcer is talking about HIV, but the couple pay no attention.)

Announcer: Today, there's a good chance you know someone with HIV. People with HIV can look just as healthy as anyone else. You can't tell if someone is infected with the virus–just by looking.

(The couple on the sofa stop making out and listen to the television announcer.)

Announcer: In fact, the person you're with right now might have HIV.

(The couple look suspiciously at each other.)

Announcer: Talk to your partner about HIV.

Voice-over Narrator: Learn how to prevent HIV infection. Call this toll-free number.

("AMERICA RESPONDS TO AIDS" logo fills the screen, followed by a toll-free phone number and the CDC identification.)

Appendix I

Transcript of CDC
PSA #6/"Missy"/:15/1991

(Scene opens with a medium shot of a woman talking. The following text appears in the lower right-hand corner of the screen: "Missy: HIV Positive.")

Character: People don't typically think of me as a person who would have HIV. But I do.

(Text fills the screen: "Anyone can get AIDS. Anyone.")

Narrator: Find out more about HIV, the virus that causes AIDS.

("AMERICA RESPONDS TO AIDS" logo fills the screen, followed by a toll-free phone number and the CDC identification.)

Appendix J

Transcript of the Oklahoma State Department of Health AIDS PSA/"Magic"/:30/1991

(Scene opens with the following voice-over narration and written text: "The best way to get the facts about HIV/AIDS is over the phone. Magic [Johnson] wants you to know the score." Then scene cuts to a medium shot of a man talking.)

Character/Narrator: Right now in Oklahoma, 10,000 men, women, and children have the HIV virus. AIDS can touch all of us. AIDS is everybody's business.

(Text fills the screen with the word "CALL," followed by a toll-free number.)

Character/Narrator: It's a free call, and the Oklahoma State Department of Health will send you a free packet about the disease, its transmission, testing, and treatment.

(The toll-free number and Oklahoma State Department of Health identification fill the screen.)

References

Aggleton, P. (1988). Evaluating health education about AIDS. In P. Aggleton, G. Hart, and P. Davies (eds.), *AIDS: Social representations, social practices* (pp. 220-36). Philadelphia: Falmer Press.

Altman, D. (1986). *AIDS in the mind of America.* Garden City: Anchor Press.

Barbedette, G. (1983). A conversation with Michel Foucault: The social triumph of the sexual will. *Christopher Street,* issue 64, pp. 36-41.

Bérubé, A. (1988). Caught in the storm: AIDS and the meaning of natural disaster. *Outlook,* Fall, pp. 8-19.

Butler, J. (1992). Sexual inversion. In D. Stanton (ed.), *Discourses of sexuality from Aristotle to AIDS* (pp. 344-61). Ann Arbor: University of Michigan Press.

Cohen, E. (1988). Foucauldian necrologies: "Gay" "politics"? politically gay? *Textual Practice, 2,* 87-101.

Crimp, D. (1988a). AIDS: Cultural analysis, cultural activism. In D. Crimp (ed.), *AIDS: Cultural analysis, cultural activism* (pp. 3-16). Cambridge: MIT Press.

_____ (1988b). How to have promiscuity in an epidemic. In D. Crimp (ed.), *AIDS: Cultural analysis, cultural activism* (pp. 237-71). Cambridge: MIT Press.

_____ (1989). Mourning and militancy. *October, 51,* 3-18.

Crimp, D., and Rolston, A. (1990). *AIDS demographics.* Seattle: Bay Press.

Dejowski, E. F. (1989). Federal restrictions on AIDS prevention efforts for gay men. *Saint Louis University Public Law Review, 8,* 275-98.

Deleuze, G. (1988). *Foucault* (S. Hand, trans.). Minneapolis: University of Minnesota Press. (Original work published in 1986.)

D'Emilio, J., and Freedman, E. (1988). *Intimate matters: A history of sexuality in America.* New York: Harper and Row.

D'Emilio, J. (1993). Capitalism and gay identity. In H. Abelove, M. Barale, and D. Halperin (eds.), *The lesbian and gay studies reader* (pp. 467-78). New York: Routledge.

Dollimore, J. (1986). The dominant and the deviant: A violent dialectic. *Critical Quarterly, 28,* 179-92.

Dreyfus, H., and Rabinow, P. (1982). *Michel Foucault: Beyond structuralism and hermeneutics.* Chicago: University of Chicago Press.

Edelman, L. (1989). The plague of discourse: Politics, literary theory, and AIDS. *South Atlantic Quarterly, 88,* 313-14.

————— (1993). Tearooms and sympathy, or, the epistemology of the water closet. In H. Abelove, M. Barale, and D. Halperin (eds.), *The lesbian and gay studies reader* (pp. 553-76). New York: Routledge.

Escoffier, J. (1985). Sexual revolution and the politics of gay identity. *Socialist Review, 15,* 119-53.

Foucault, M. (1973). *Madness and civilization: A history of insanity in the age of reason* (rev. ed.) (R. Howard, trans.). New York: Random House. (Original work published in 1961.)

————— (1973). *The order of things: An archaeology of the human sciences* (rev. ed.). New York: Vintage Books. (Original work published in 1966.)

————— (1972). *The archaeology of knowledge and the discourse on language* (S. Smith, trans.). New York: Pantheon Books. (Original work published in 1969.)

————— (1979). *Discipline and punish: The birth of the prison* (rev. ed.) (A. Sheridan, trans.). New York: Vintage Books. (Original work published in 1975.)

————— (1990). *The history of sexuality: An introduction, vol. 1* (rev. ed.) (R. Hurley, trans.). New York: Vintage Books. (Original work published in 1976.)

————— (1990). *The history of sexuality: The use of pleasure, vol. 2* (rev. ed.) (R. Hurley, trans.). New York: Vintage Books. (Original work published in 1984.)

————— (1988). *The history of sexuality: The care of the self, vol. 3* (rev. ed.) (R. Hurley, trans.). New York: Vintage Books. (Original work published in 1984.)

Frye, N. (1973). *The anatomy of criticism: Four essays* (rev. ed.). Princeton: Princeton University Press.

Gallagher, B., and Wilson, A. (1984, August 7). Michel Foucault, an interview: Sex, power, and the politics of identity. *The Advocate,* pp. 26-30 and 50.

Garner, J., Hardesty, C. L., and Wenk, D. (1992). Religion, attitudes, and support for rights for lesbians and gay men. Unpublished manuscript, Department of Sociology, University of Oklahoma, Norman.

Gilman, S. (1988). *Disease and representation: Images of illness from madness to AIDS.* Ithaca: Cornell University Press.

Grover, J. Z. (1988). AIDS: Keywords. In D. Crimp (ed.), *AIDS: Cultural analysis, cultural activism* (pp. 17-30). Cambridge: MIT Press.

Halperin, D. (1993). Is there a history of sexuality? In H. Abelove, M. Barale, and D. Halperin (eds.), *The lesbian and gay studies reader* (pp. 416-31). New York: Routledge. (Originally published in 1989.)

Hammerstein, O. (1943). *Oklahoma!* New York: Random House.

Hanson, E. (1991). Undead. In D. Fuss (ed.), *Inside/out: Lesbian theories, gay theories* (pp. 324-40). New York: Routledge.

Hill, S. (1992). Personal interview, November 25.

Hinton, M. (1992, December 15). State health department announces AIDS director. *The Daily Oklahoman,* p. 13.

Homans, H., and Aggleton, P. (1988). Health education, HIV infection and AIDS. In P. Aggleton and H. Homans (eds.), *Social aspects of AIDS* (pp. 154-76). Philadelphia: Falmer Press.

Hughes, W. (1993, July 20). Feeling mighty real: Disco as discourse and discipline. *The Village Voice,* pp. 7-11 and 21.

Hunt, L. (1992). Foucault's subject in the *History of Sexuality.* In D. Stanton (ed.), *Discourses of sexuality from Aristotle to AIDS* (pp. 78-93). Ann Arbor: University of Michigan Press.

Kayal, P. (1993). *Bearing witness: Gay men's health crisis and the politics of AIDS.* Boulder: Westview Press, Inc.

Kelley, J. A., Lawrence, J. S., Stevenson, L. Y., Hauth, A. C., Kalichman, S. C., Diaz, Y. E., Brasfield, T. L., Koob, J. J., and Morgan, M. G. (1992). Community AIDS/HIV risk reduction: The effects of endorsements by popular people in three cities. *American Journal of Public Health, 82,* 1483-89.

Kirby, R. (1992). Personal interview, December 4.

Landers, T. (1988). Bodies and antibodies: A crisis in representation. *The Independent, 11,* 18-24.

Mahon, M. (1992). *Foucault's Nietzschean genealogy: Truth, power, and the subject.* Albany, NY: State University of New York Press.

Marcus, E. (1992). *Making history: The struggle for gay and lesbian rights–1945-1990.* New York: HarperCollins.

Marshall, S. (1990). Picturing deviancy. In T. Boffin and S. Gupta (eds.), *Ecstatic antibodies: Resisting the AIDS mythology* (pp. 19-37). London: Rivers Oram Press.

_____ (1991). The contemporary political use of gay history and the Third Reich. In Bad Object Choices (ed.), *How do I look: Queer film and video* (pp. 65-101). Seattle: Bay Press.

McAllister, M. (1992). AIDS, medicalization, and the news media. In T. Edgar, M. A. Fitzpatrick, and V. Freimuth (eds.), *AIDS: A Communication Perspective* (pp. 195-222). Hillsdale, NJ: Lawrence Erlbaum Associates.

McGrath, R. (1990). Dangerous liaisons: Health, disease, and representation. In S. Watney and S. Gupta (eds.), *Ecstatic antibodies: Resisting the AIDS mythology* (pp. 142-55). London: Rivers Oram Press.

Meyer, R. (1993). Robert Mapplethorpe and the discipline of photography. In H. Abelove, M. Barale, and D. Halperin (eds.), *The gay and lesbian studies reader* (pp. 360-80). New York: Routledge.

Miller, J. (1993). *The passion of Michel Foucault.* New York: Simon & Schuster.

Nyitray, A. (1992). Personal interview, November 18.

Nyitray, A. (1995). Personal interview, October 20.

Niekerk, A., and van der Meer, T. (1989). Homosexuality, which homosexuality. In A. Niekerk & T. Meer (eds.), *Homosexuality, which homosexuality* (pp. 5-12). London: GMP Publishers.

Nietzsche, F. (1981). *Beyond good and evil* (rev. ed.) (R. Hollingdale, trans.). New York: Penguin. (Original work published in 1886.)

NO/AIDS Task Force (1992). *Mansex: Do it right.* Pamphlet on Safer Sex for Gay Men. (Originally available from NO/AIDS Task Force, 1407 Decatur St., New Orleans, LA 70116-2010).

Nunokawa, J. (1991). "All the sad young men": AIDS and the work of mourning. In D. Fuss (ed.), *Inside out: Lesbian theories, gay theories* (pp. 311-23). New York: Routledge.

Oklahoma State Department of Health (1992a). *Considering an Oklahoma cruise? Wanting to sail uncharted waters?* Pamphlet on Safer Sex for Gay Men. (Available from the Oklahoma State Department of Health HIV-STD Service, Mail Drop 0308, 1000 N.E. 10th St., Oklahoma City, OK 73117-1299.)

Oklahoma State Department of Health (1992b). *Oklahoma HIV/ AIDS Surveillance Newsletter.* (The HIV/STD newsletter is available from the Oklahoma State Department of Health, HIV-STD Service, Mail Drop 0308, 1000 N.E. 10th St., Oklahoma City, OK 73117-1299.)

Palacios-Jimenez, L., and Shernoff, M. (1989). *Eroticizing safer sex: A psychoeducational workshop approach to safer sex education* (2nd ed.). New York: Gay Men's Health Crisis.

Patton, C. (1985). *Sex and germs: The politics of AIDS.* Boston: South End Press.

———— (1988). AIDS: Lessons from the gay community. *Feminist Review, 30,* 105-11.

———— (1989). Resistance and the erotic. In P. Aggleton, G. Hart, and P. Davies (eds.), *AIDS: Social representations, social practices* (pp. 237-51). Philadelphia: Falmer Press.

———— (1990a). What science knows: Formations of AIDS knowledges. In P. Aggleton, P. Davies, and G. Hart (eds.), *AIDS: Individual, cultural, and policy dimensions* (pp. 1-18). New York: Falmer Press.

———— (1990b). *Inventing AIDS.* New York: Routledge.

_____ (1991). Safe sex and the pornographic vernacular. In Bad Object Choices (ed.), *How do I look: Queer film and video* (pp. 31-63). Seattle: Bay Press.

Prater, L. (1993). Personal interview, January 22.

Ringer, J. (ed.) (1994). *Queer words, queer images: Communication and the construction of homosexuality.* New York: New York University Press.

Rubin, G. (1993). Thinking sex: Notes for a radical theory of the politics of sexuality. In H. Abelove, M. Barale, and D. Halperin (eds.), *The lesbian and gay studies reader* (pp. 3-44). New York: Routledge. (Originally published in 1984.)

Singer, L. (1993). *Erotic welfare: Sexual theory and politics in the age of epidemic.* New York: Routledge.

Schecter, S. (1991). *The AIDS notebooks.* Albany, NY: State University of New York Press.

Schernoff, M., and Palacios-Jimenez, L. (1988). AIDS: Prevention is the only vaccine available: An AIDS prevention educational program. *Journal of Social Work and Human Sexuality, 6,* 135-50.

Seidman, S. (1988). Transfiguring sexual identity: AIDS and the contemporary construction of homosexuality. *Social text: theory/culture/ideology, 7,* 187-209.

Shapiro, M. J. (1981). *Language and political understanding: The politics of discursive practices.* New Haven: Yale University Press.

_____ (1984). Literary production as politicizing practice. In M. J. Shapiro (ed.), *Language and politics* (pp. 215-53). New York: New York University Press.

Smithson, D. (1992). Personal interview, December 23.

Smithson, D. and Steeves, T. (1992). Personal interview, December 18.

Stall, R. D., Coates, T. J., and Hoff, C. (1988). Behavioral risk reduction for HIV infection among gay and bisexual men: A review of results from the United States. *American Psychologist, 43,* 878-85.

Strong, T. (1984). Language and nihilism. In M. Shapiro (ed.),

Language and politics (pp. 81-107). New York: New York University Press.

Treichler, P. (1988). AIDS, homophobia, and biomedical discourse: An epidemic of signification. In D. Crimp (ed.), *AIDS: Cultural analysis, cultural activism* (pp. 31-70). Cambridge: MIT Press.

Watney, S. (1987a). *Policing desire: Pornography, AIDS and the media.* Minneapolis: University of Minnesota Press.

Watney, S. (1987b). AIDS: The cultural agenda. *Radical America,* 21, pp. 49-53.

_____ (1988a). The spectacle of AIDS. In D. Crimp (ed.), *AIDS: Cultural analysis, cultural activism* (pp. 71-86). Cambridge: MIT Press.

_____ (1988b). AIDS, "moral panic" theory and homophobia. In P. Aggleton and H. Homans (eds.), *Social aspects of AIDS* (pp. 52-64). New York: Falmer Press.

_____ (1989a). The subject of AIDS. In P. Aggleton, G. Hart, and P. Davies (eds.), *AIDS: Social representations, social practices* (pp. 64-73). New York: Falmer Press.

_____ (1989b). Psychoanalysis, sexuality and AIDS. In S. Shepard and M. Wallis (eds.), *Coming on strong: Gay politics and culture* (pp. 22-38). London: Unwin Hyman.

_____ (1990). Safe sex as community practice. In P. Aggleton, P. Davies, and G. Hart (eds.), *AIDS: Individual, cultural, and policy dimensions* (pp. 19-34). New York: Falmer Press.

Weeks, J. (1985). *Sexuality and its discontents: Meanings, myths & modern sexualities.* London: Routledge.

_____ (1989a). Against nature. In A. Niekerk and T. van der Meer (eds.), *Homosexuality, which homosexuality?* (pp. 199-214). London: GMP Publishers.

_____ (1989b). AIDS: The intellectual agenda. In P. Aggleton, G. Hart, and P. Davis (eds.), *AIDS: Social representations, social practices* (pp. 1-20). New York: Falmer Press.

Williamson, J. (1989). Every virus tells a story: The meanings of HIV and AIDS. In E. Carter and S. Watney (eds.), *Taking liberties: AIDS and cultural politics* (pp. 69-80). London: Serpent's Tail.

Yingling, T. (1991). AIDS in America: Postmodern governance, identity, and experience. In D. Fuss (ed.), *Inside out: Lesbian theories, gay theories* (pp. 291-310). New York: Routledge.

Index